943.84 EIL   COPY 1
Eilenbers, Anna.   OCLC
Breaking my silence. 11.95

1986

Virginia Public Library
Virginia, Minnesota

Breaking My Silence

BREAKING MY SILENCE

by Anna Eilenberg

VIRGINIA PUBLIC LIBRARY
VIRGINIA, MINNESOTA

SHENGOLD PUBLISHERS, INC.
NEW YORK

ISBN 0-88400-112-1
Library of Congress Catalog Card Number: 84-72760
Copyright © 1985 by Anna Eilenberg

All rights reserved

Published by Shengold Publishers Inc.
New York, N.Y. 10036

Printed in the United States of America

*To my late husband, Avigdor,
who encouraged me to record the
suffering, struggle and hope of our everyday life
under the Nazi yoke.*

*In loving memory of
my father, mother and brother,
who perished at the hands of the Nazis.*

Contents

Preface 7
Prologue to My Dear Children 9
1. Lodz 13
2. Personal History 17
3. A New Era 19
4. The Ghetto 37
5. Resistance 70
6. Sanctification of the Divine Name—Self-Sacrifice 80
7. Auschwitz 93
8. Liberation—9 May 1945 112
9. Aftermath 122

Many thanks to Professor Yehuda Shamir for his guidance in my studies towards the B.A and Masters degrees, and whose thought-provoking lectures provided the stimulus for the creation of this work.

I should also like to express my gratitude to Beit Lochamei Haghetaot for providing me with the pictures for this book.

Preface

The nature of the survivors of the Holocaust is imprisoned by guilt feelings. We live in our shattered memories; we live a life of self-condemnation. We ask why we survived while our dear ones were brutally killed. If we were able to share our feelings, our torments with others who could understand, our burden would be lighter. However, it is characteristic of our present society that we meet with little understanding. Often we meet with embarrassed silence. Consequently, we ourselves resort to silence.

When I first enrolled in a class entitled Creative Writing at Barry University in 1980, my objectives were not clear. Now I find that this was an exceptionally fortunate decision, for I found the way to break my silence with the help of my teacher, Dr. Nathalie Marshall-Nadel.

I had never done any serious writing before the class started. I was not sure that I could handle the subjects that I wanted to write about. I expressed these doubts to my teacher. She assured me that I stood a good chance of succeeding. Her encouragement put me at ease.

On the first day of class the students were asked to start writing their autobiographies. I was thrown off balance. Who would want to know what I had to say about myself? What could I say that would be of interest to the teacher and others? And if I did write about myself, how could they understand? My head started to pound and my palms began to sweat. I picked up my pen, but I could not write anything. The pen kept slipping from my shaking hands. I became aware that the teacher was noticing my discomfort. I forced myself to write.

I wondered if she could sense what I wanted to say. Now I became eager to describe the images of my past. Like a film, my yesterdays unreeled before me. I saw my father and my mother, my brother and my sister and my whole family. They were so young and so beautiful that I felt I wanted to join them again.

Then I looked around the reality of the classroom with its twenty-one other students and I wanted to run out into the garden beyond. Embarrassment was the only thing that held me still.

The teacher instructed the students to read what they had written. When the student next to me finished reading her composition, I closed my notebook and said I would not read mine. Dr. Marshall-Nadel asked my why. I stammered that I just could not. She just looked at me with tender and smiling eyes. I felt naked and realized she could see through my resistance. I stood up with clenched fists and started to read.

It took all my strength to control my emotions. I felt that each word tore at a part of myself. The words danced around on the pages, but I kept reciting from memory. When I sat down, exhausted, I felt the understanding coming from the eyes of the other students and the teacher.

From then on Nathalie—as I learned to call her—encouraged me to continue. "Write *every* day. Write until the whole story is on paper. Others will read and understand what you have to say." When I faltered, she said, "Just put your recollections on paper and don't worry about your English—we can correct that later. You have to write for the sake of others who are still silent and for yourself."

She was right. I still do not know if she realized the magnitude of her influence over me. Her encouragement was balm to my soul. She commented on the turbulent pages with great understanding. Gradually I started to open up; I started to share my deepest memories.

It is obvious to me that until I started to write, I had not been able to handle the experience of the Holocaust. The injustices and cruelties I experienced created knots of resistance in my being. Now when the nightmares came, I got up and went to the typewriter. Often the pages became drenched with tears, but I felt what I was doing was necessary, for myself and for others, the living as well as the dead. For the dead would be remembered, and if the living knew how it was perhaps they would be strong enough next time not to permit such a tragedy to happen again.

Prologue to My Dear Children

There comes a time when one cannot maintain calm and silence. There comes a time when obligations must be carried out even at the risk of opening old wounds. I feel an obligation to write of events that I have kept in darkness for forty years. Six million people were obliterated. All of them were innocent of any wrong doing. They were slaughtered because they were Jews.

The phenomenon of the Holocaust surpasses human understanding. To this day no satisfactory explanation has been found as to why it was allowed to happen. Did the free world have a part in it directly or indirectly. What caused its failure to act when the killings took place in such an organized manner and over such a long period of time? How could the world stand by, watch and witness, and be silent?

My wish, dear children, is that you seriously study the events of the Holocaust. Its history can be verified by live witnesses, though time for us, the survivors, is running out. In the future you will have to rely on documents alone. The records and evidence already compiled tell such an incredible story that for many it verges on the realm of fantasy. People who are not survivors say that imagination and exaggeration have distorted the truth. Perhaps they say this so that they can stop believing the atrocities really occurred. But if they do so, the Holocaust could be allowed to happen again! As long as there are still survivors who can personally attest to the Nazi crimes, your study will be deeper and more far-reaching. My story is just one of many.

When Hitler came to power, the ground for his actions was well prepared. The minds of the illiterate and the unenlightened Germans were already fired with hatred of the Jews by earlier anti-Semites. As Hitler assumed control over Germany, he used this hatred to the maximum benefit of his regime. His stated goal, next in importance to conquering the world, was to remove every Jew from the face of the Earth. For this purpose he used all available media of the time. Through radio, press and loudspeakers he aroused the lowest instincts of his countrymen. He gathered thousands of people into giant halls, stripped them of individuality and identity, and with thundering speeches molded them hypnotically into a single bestial mass. They became cogs in his giant machine of conquest. The property and labor of the Jews was taken to run this infernal machine.

History has taught us that man can be a very dangerous creature. One segment of mankind can destroy another in a programmed and callous manner while rationalizing and justifying its actions. The Holocaust is the most monstrous example of this. We have to be on guard not to let this happen again! We have learned—though much too late—the importance of interpreting events early and without illusion. We know now that being alert to happenings all over the world might be the key to life and death.

The existence of a nation depends on its continuity, and its continuity depends on the transmission of its history for the understanding of future generations. If we do not transmit our history of the Holocaust, we break the chain of our being.

How do the people in our free democratic society react to the Holocaust? An incident which happened to me during a symposium may shed some light on the experiences other survivors have had. The topic of the symposium was: Did the people of the free world live up to their responsibility during the Nazi Era? I stood up and said some of the people of America knew that there was a merciless slaughter of European Jews under way and yet did nothing to stop it. To prove my point I presented a newspaper article which revealed that President Roosevelt had concealed the full truth about the death factories of Chelmno, Auschwitz, and Treblinka from the American people. He withheld documents proving that mass exterminations of Jews in gas chambers was a fact. He even reduced the Jewish immigration quota to the United States when those who escaped the Holocaust sorely needed refuge.

The audience at the symposium was somewhat irritated by my words. They gave the impression that this was an unpleasant topic. One of them asked, "What is the use of dwelling on what happened in the past?"

I persisted in spite of the pain their indifference caused. I maintained that our past could have been entirely different if people had protested instead of being silent bystanders. Why didn't they write to their elected representatives or demonstrate to show their concern? A sincere expression of concern might have changed the President's policies. One young woman tried to convince me that her parents did not know. I told her those who had made it a point to know what was going on in Europe were aware of the truth. I heard murmurs of "She is over-reacting," "She is over-sensitive!" I produced two legal-size sheets of paper listing articles and reports from *The New York Times* dating from March 4, 1933, to May 6, 1945, all referring to the plight of European Jews. How can one condone ignorance of such magnitude? I asked if such ignorance on the part of Americans was justifiable. No one answered. I had to continue, "If we learn from our past, we have to admit to ourselves the tremendous mistakes we made. We have to accept the truth that the free world was indifferent to the plight of six million Jews. The guilt of the silent bystanders must be understood and accepted so that nothing like the Holocaust will ever happen again."

We Jews, too, have learned a lesson. We must be more alert and less naive. If we had been able to believe that one man could galvanize other men into burning victims alive without qualm, more of us could have been saved.

I know my reaction to the Holocaust has to be entirely different from yours. You cannot see into my memory as I visualize those horror filled days. You cannot see the mountains of dead bodies that I see even today. You cannot hear the cries from the death factories that still linger in my ears even as we speak. I can find no peace from these sights and sounds. All those innocent lives trapped in a net of horror are still a part of the bedrock of my memory. Of course, this pain is not my pain alone. There are many like myself who have kept silent in order to begin life again and raise our children without hatred. But I can contain my pain no longer.

Our martyrs have entrusted us, the survivors, with a mission to spread their last message: *Remember! Remember us and what was done to us by the Nazis*! If we do not transmit their message, we transgress the command of our martyrs. If we do not speak out, we betray their memory. And that memory is their grandest monument.

Dear children, as I am about to tell my own story, you must understand why I cannot be calm and composed when I speak of the

Holocaust. You may be correct in blaming me for not enlightening you at an earlier time. My only explanation is you were so young and I wanted to spare you the knowledge of the agony and suffering of your family. Now you are adults. You have children of your own. Now is the time to learn fully this tragic chapter in our history.

I realize that some people shy away from the study of the Holocaust because they are afraid of their own reactions to such horror. They are afraid they cannot handle the complex mixture of sorrow and guilt. Perhaps they are afraid they may lack empathy for those who endured these terrible experiences. Whatever the reason for their fear, they must learn what really happened and so also learn about themselves.

The unknown is frightening. Lack of knowledge about any subject may cause misinterpretation and misunderstanding. If people would familiarize themselves with the events of the Holocaust, our *Shoah*, they could accept it as a part of our history and then they would learn how to cope with this knowledge. For just as one cannot run away from himself, so, too, one cannot run away from his past.

For us and for future generations, the most important thing to remember is that the most fitting monument for our six million martyrs is our shared memory of what happened. The Nazi aim was to destroy the Jews without leaving a trace. Had Hitler's "Final Solution" been successful, no Jew would have survived. It is our obligation to remember this, and to transmit this memory, document by document, to present and future generations.

1. Lodz

Lodz! The city of my childhood hopes and dreams. The place where I was born, raised, planned a happy future, sought to realize the beauty of life. All this evaporated. My youthful hopes withered away before they had a chance to bloom. My dreams vanished in an ocean of anguish and pain before my very eyes, and before I could understand the real meaning of life.

Lodz was also the city where my father and my grandfather were born and had lived all their lives. Still vivid in my imagination are the stories my grandfather told me about the dense forest near where his house stood. It was he who first told me how the little town of Lodz in a very short time grew into the second largest city in Poland. In the early nineteenth century, it had contained only 800 inhabitants, but when the Industrial Revolution reached Poland, Lodz was chosen to be a major industrial center. With the introduction of Western technology, vigorous development got under way, and one of the pioneer programs was underwritten by German and Jewish entrepreneurs from the West. With the establishment of a particular major textile center—for manufacturing cotton, linen, and woolen goods—Lodz became the most important industrial city in Poland.

Along with this rapid development, the population grew. From 800 souls in 1820 it swelled to 50,500 in 1872. In 1876 the people of the city numbered 80,000, and at the outbreak of World War II, half a million! It was then the second largest city, in both population and importance, after Warsaw, the capital.

Jewish energy was largely responsible for the rapid growth of Lodz. The first textile factories were built and operated in the first half of the nineteenth century by a group of Jewish weavers. From then on Jewish participation in the city's industrial development grew steadily. In 1872, half of Lodz's population was Jewish. The Jews worked side by side with non-Jews, each person to a loom. Power for the machines was provided by one central station, and when looms were vacated by observant Jews on the Sabbath, costly power was lost. This created a dilemma for the mostly Jewish owners of the factories, who were expected by the Jewish community to hire Jewish workers. Israel Poznanski solved the problem by setting up special factories for Sabbath observers.

Provision was also made for the educational needs of the Jewish community. Before the outbreak of World War II, when Jews constituted more than a third of the Lodz population, many of the students and teachers in the public schools were Jewish. There were thirty-one elementary schools for Jewish children with 17,902 students, twelve Cheders (Jewish religious boys' schools) with 1,452 students, and ten Jewish high schools with 1,861 students, to which were attached ten elementary schools with 1,112 students. This made for a total of sixty-three schools with 22,337 Jewish students.

In Lodz the Jewish community had established many charitable organizations to provide for the needy. There were old-age homes and homes for orphans. There were well organized Zionist organizations, labor organizations, and religious organizations, as well as Hassidic groups and non-Hassidic Mitnagdim groups organized for studying Torah. Jewish newspapers were published daily. The Jews constituted a vibrant, productive, cohesive social body which functioned normally, until the rise of Hitler.

With the rise of Hitler, however, the situation began to change. The security of the Jews of Lodz deteriorated. Organized murders occurred from time to time. In 1934, local fascists, running on a platform of making Lodz free of Jews, won an overwhelming majority in the municipal elections. This was the prelude to nightmare.

The Nazi invasion of Poland in September, 1939, brought the largest and most vital Jewish community of Europe, numbering more than three million, into Hitler's grasp. To carry out their stated "Solution to the Jewish Question," the Nazis began by robbing the Jews of their possessions, then used the people for forced labor till the last drop of their strength was gone, and finally, annihilated them.

To achieve their goals effectively and speedily, the Nazis established ghettos. The first of these was Ghetto Lodz. After haphazard lootings, plunderings, robbings, and killings, the Jews of Lodz were herded into the poorest, filthiest, and most neglected Baluty section of the city, where 60,000 Jews already lived.

During the period of transition all the gentiles living in the designated ghetto area were ordered to move out, while the Jews from other parts of Lodz moved in. The Jews had to leave their homes without delay. They were not permitted to take with them any tools, machines, or instruments, not even their own furniture or merchandise for their stores. They were not even allowed to take all their clothing.

On February 8, 1940 Ghetto Lodz was established, and on May 1 of that same year it was sealed off. Within its walls 180,000 Jews were imprisoned, pressed into an area of one and a half square miles. The fate of these Jews was not in doubt. And every day brought their doom closer.

Security control of the ghetto was entrusted to the Gestapo, while police functions were given over to the Krippo, or Criminal Police. Under the German mayor of Lodz, a ghetto administration was established, which was subordinated to the German mayor. His function was to gradually deprive the Jewish population of all its property, exploiting its labor potential, and eventually liquidating them. On October 13, 1939 Mordechai Chaim Rumkowski became the *Elteste*, or chief administrator of the Jews. The circumstances surrounding Rumkowski's appointment are obscure to this very day. Rumkowski made an agreement with the Germans whereby they were to provision the ghetto and he was to turn over to them Jewish possessions and supply them with Jewish labor. In the opinion of many, he chose to make a personal advantage of the general Jewish disaster. But Rumkowski, the Jewish "dictator of the ghetto," as he was called, may have deceived himself about the true nature of the role he played.

In any case he controlled the property of the ghetto and he was its judge. In his power rested the fate of all of its inhabitants. When demonstrations broke out, he could call on German troops to shoot down the demonstrators.

All of the Jewish community were placed under Rumkowski's control or those whom he appointed. He was also authorized by the Germans to impose a tax on the ghetto inhabitants. One of the pillars of Rumkowski's belief was that work would save the ghetto. Accordingly, on May 13, 1940, two weeks after the ghetto was sealed off, Rumkowski submitted a letter to the German mayor informing him that he had completed the registration of 14,850 skilled workers. To this he attached a list of over seventy articles which the ghetto would produce for the benefit of the German economy. Soon afterward, shops and factories, called "resorts," were established in the ghetto to produce these goods, which were supplemented by expropriated property which the Jewish inhabitants somehow had managed to save.

Thanks to Rumkowski's organizational efficiency and his drive to continuously please the Germans, Ghetto Lodz came to be considered an "exemplary ghetto." In no other ghetto was there such colossal productivity. It is quite possible that this was the reason the Lodz Ghetto was the last to be liquidated. Nevertheless, deportations of Jews to unknown destinations, which began even before the ghetto was established, continued. Evidently the Germans felt that extermination by starvation, hard labor, and epidemic was too slow although more than 43,000 people died of hunger, tuberculosis, dysentery, and typhoid fever, in Ghetto Lodz between 1940 and 1944. To hasten the process, they set up a death camp in Chelmno, thirty miles away. The creation of this camp in 1941 opened a new chapter in the history of my people, of which I am now prepared to give my personal witness.

2. Personal History

In my memory my childhood and my early teenage years are an isle of peace, happiness, and delight. My father was a scribe who copied the Bible on scrolls of parchment. Every letter of his hand was written with the greatest devotion to the Almighty. Every morning, before starting his work, he immersed himself in a ritual bath, to purify his body for its holy task. He also learned portions of Talmud as spiritual preparation for the writing of scrolls, phylacteries, and mezuzoth. Whenever he paused from his writing, during the day or evening, he would turn to the study of Torah. His piety and learning together with his most beautiful handwriting caused many people, especially Hassidim, to seek him out. To be sure of obtaining his work, they paid him in advance, which was very good—but also very bad. For we were poor and the money was needed. And because it was badly needed, it was used. As a result my father was always in debt.

My mother was a physically weak person, but a spiritually strong one, and a very devoted wife. Desiring to help father in earning a livelihood, she established a workshop for artistic weaving. I was eight years old at the time. In the beginning she worked by herself, but later on she took on a few employees. The workshop was in our apartment, separated from my father's scriptorium by a folding partition. At the far end of this room were two beds, a closet on one wall and a sofa on the other. When night came, the shop was folded away, and the beds were set up for sleeping. Our apartment also included a large kitchen, which was partitioned so that half comprised an entrance hall and half could be used as an extra bedroom, if needed.

Now, when I think back to those days, I see that we must have been very crowded; however, then, I did not feel so. Besides my parents and myself, my older brother Benjamin and my younger sister Salusia occupied this small space.

We were a happy family, not rich but warm-hearted, cheerful and harmonious. Between my parents there was always love and mutual respect. I grew up in a loving, supportive atmosphere, a carefree and joyful child. Then, at the end of vacation, after my graduation from elementary school, the war broke out. On September 1, 1939, the Nazis marched into Poland, and three days later our city lay crushed under the Nazi heel. Our fate was sealed. My happy childhood suddenly was swept away; my youth was over before it began. I knew my future would be very different from my past.

3. A New Era

For one thing, I would have to adjust to the idea of not going to high school, of which I had dreamed. Happy school days now belonged in another lifetime. The dreary day-to-day struggle to stay alive took their place in the face of the swift changes happening all around me. I felt crushed, as if the world was closing in on me. Although I wasn't alone in this situation, I felt lost. I sought refuge then in a world of illusion, the world of beauty and perfection found only in books.

The real world around me was crumbling. Fear, death, and horror were part of our everyday life. Every morning I asked myself two questions: how could I go on living and why did we Jews deserve such punishment? Alongside these troubling questions, was the fearful premonition that our present hardships would not be the end, that worse times lay ahead of us. However, in the early days of the war I could still think. I could still plan in my mind that I would fight, that I would not yield to circumstances, that I would not let myself be crushed. I would be strong and I would resist. Books like Romain Roland's *The Enchanted Soul* and his *John Kristof* became weapons in my struggle. The latter work was in four volumes, and to buy it was beyond my means. However, when my cousin fled to Warsaw as the Germans were approaching Lodz, she gave me these and other books as a present.

In those early days of the war I was still able to create my own world; yet even then I could not fully shut out the reality of my surroundings.

In the middle of December, 1939, rumors started to spread that the Jews would be forced to leave the city, that Lodz was to be made *Judenrein*, free of Jews. At night these rumors occupied my mind and did not let me fall asleep. I thought: Free of Jews? But then we would have to move. But where to?

I didn't comprehend yet that moving would not be the worst of it and that we would have to endure the impossible. I looked around the house and thought: Will we be able to take our furniture with us? Will I be able to read my books? Will I be allowed to take them with me? Even then I felt a little uncomfortable carrying a book with me whenever I knew that I would have to spend a long time in a line. People would give me strange and unfriendly looks when they saw me reading while I waited. But I couldn't just stand there and think about our miserable situation. The fact that I had to wait in line to get a piece of bread was unbearable enough. However, when I heard, "Look at this stupid girl—she needs stories now!" I was hurt. In all honesty, it wasn't stories I needed, but something to lean on, something to hold on to, and my books gave me that.

The onslaught of the Nazis was sudden and fearful. They came like a cloud of green locusts, like a horde of brutes in human form. Masses of flesh and steel, a stream of thunderous terror in dawn heavy with foreboding. This was how that early sunless morning of September 5, 1939, when the German oppressor took possession of our city of Lodz, seemed. Even the smallest child among us could feel the cloud of abysmal evil and disaster descending upon us. We were enveloped, as doomed to destruction as the sinful generation of the Flood.

The city went numb. Only the roaring noise of cannon fire could be heard. It seemed to have silenced all life in town. Everybody froze in fear, listening to the sounds of approaching shells and heavy vehicles. The Germans were closing in on us. Then one could distinctly hear the marching troops, the rhythmic tramp of horse artillery, as the Germans entered our city.

The first days of the war brought thousands of refugees to our city. They looked for shelter in our midst. In the chilly preday darkness of dawn, parents and children clustered together in the obscurity of the cobblestone yards. When the morning finally came and the sun started its slide over the horizon, we Jews joined the refugees in their despair and lamentation.

Some of these unfortunate people were wounded, others were in a state of shock. They told us of their terrible experiences on their way to our town—of friends and relatives killed while fleeing or left on the road to die. All of them were exhausted, dirty, thirsty and hungry. Despite the tales of the refugees, showing the uselessness of running, many of our men decided to flee, because there was a rumor that all men in the city would be shot. They poured onto the roads without plan or destination, some to vanish forever, others to return soon afterwards, telling of soldiers firing at running people from low-flying airplanes. In truth, there was no place to run.

One day, in my house, it seemed as if the walls were closing in on me, and some inner force, stronger than myself, pushed me out into the street. There I was caught up in the excitement of a crowd watching a procession of marching German soldiers. I was too young and still too secure to be frightened. I ran after the marchers, and when I got to Piotrkowska Street, stopped at an elevated spot to get a better view of our conquerers. To this day I cannot explain what I wanted to see. I just know that what happened next shattered something in me forever.

As the soldiers marched, they now began to sing: "*Whenn Judenblut von Messer spritzt / Dann geht's nochmal so gut!*" I knew enough German to understand the words. When Jewish blood from the knife spurts / then all goes doubly well! I felt a sudden chill. Then I noticed that our neighbor, Mr. Schultz was singing this song along with the soldiers, and a frightening tremor seized my whole body. He was one of a few men wearing a German militia uniform with a shiny black swastika band. For the first time in my life I knew the meaning of utter despair.

Although Mr. Schultz was a Pole, my parents considered him our friend. He liked to spend time in my father's company. He also enjoyed my mother's cooking. He had regularly delivered to her rolls of fabric from the time my mother had started her shop. He usually came on Friday and often joined us for lunch. Now, seeing him in his German uniform, I realized that he must have been our enemy all along. I pushed myself through the dense crowd and started for home. The main avenues were filled with the marchers and spectators. I took the side streets.

I had walked hardly five minutes when I heard shots. Then I saw two German soldiers pulling a man out of his house, throwing him to the ground and savagely beating him over the head and body until he fell unconscious. A little farther down the street a cluster of military men were walking and shooting randomly into windows of homes. Violence was all around me. I was terrified. My knees shook, but I somehow kept on walking, going faster and faster until I was running and hiding whenever I saw an open gateway. I was trembling uncontrollably. I had to stop and catch my breath and steady my feet. Then I decided not to run anymore. I straightened up, and without looking right or left, resumed my walk with a sure step. Exhausted and bewildered, I gratefully reached home.

The following day Jews experienced indescribable terror. Their shops were looted, their homes were plundered, and many were killed there and in the streets. The Nazis rounded up still other Jews, beat them mercilessly, hurled them into trucks, and drove them off to clean stables with their bare hands. Under threat of bayonet and rifle-shot, they worked day and night without rest and without food. Some of these unfortunates died, others were maimed; all who came back were broken and sick. Horror and panic spread through the town. Jews did not venture to leave their homes and kept their doors tightly shut.

My mother had a weak heart, and the fear and excitement she now experienced caused her severe chest pains. My father was aware of the danger he exposed himself to by going into the street, but he also knew that my mother needed immediate medical attention. He went to the nearest drugstore to call a doctor. I was afraid that something might happen to my father, and that I should have gone with him, but I could not leave mother alone. From the moment he left the house I did not move away from the window. I thought, if I had gone with him, I could have made sure that Nazis were not lurking around any corner. They were looking for men and did not yet care so much about girls. They usually stationed their trucks away from the area in which they did their hunting. Most of the time when my father or brother had to go out into the street, I walked a half a block in front of them to make sure that they would not be getting into danger. The drugstore my father was supposed to call from was near our house; yet I was frightened.

I was still peering through the shuttered window, when I heard shots in the courtyard. At the same moment I saw Mr. Schultz running with a rifle pointed at the entrance to our staircase. In his haste, he tripped on a long, thin piece of wood that stuck out from a pile of boards belonging to the bakery, which was located on the right side of the staircase. Mr. Schultz fell face down and blood gushed from his hands and face. I do not know who called for help, but people came to take him away immediately.

Dumbfounded, I tried to figure out what had happened when I saw father running home. He came into the apartment and, trembling and speechless, fell on the bed. Only after some minutes could he tell us what he had just experienced. While waiting to make his call he saw storm troopers rounding up people. When the truck was full and started to move away, he felt relief and thanked God that he had been spared arrest. He made his call, left the drugstore and rushed home.

Once in the street, he sensed that he was being followed. He accelerated his pace. So did the person behind him. Realizing that he would soon be overtaken, he started to run. My father was only a couple of steps from our gateway when he heard his name called, and then shots. The shots narrowly missed him as he leapt into the gateway. From there he dashed up the staircase, taking three and four steps at a time, until he reached the attic.

It was then my father knew beyond doubt who his attacker was. He heard Mr. Schultz's voice calling for him on each landing of the staircase until he reached the attic. As luck would have it, at that particular time the attic was completely empty of drying laundry. Only slack hanging lines were dangling from the ceiling. Mr. Schultz had a view of the whole attic at once. There were many storage areas behind doors in the sloping edges of the ceiling. These were full. Every tenant of the house had an assigned space, and had crammed it with extra possessions. From behind the entrance door where he was hidden, father could hear Mr. Schultz opening the doors of the storage places one by one, banging, ripping, and shoving things out. In his fury, he banged his head against the ceiling, and outraged, he ran down the stairs into the yard. He was heading directly for our apartment when he stumbled over the piece of wood and fell.

By the time father finished describing his experience, he was almost completely calm. He told my brother, my sister and me to leave the apartment immediately. "Just take your overcoats, and run! Run for your lives! Mr. Schultz will surely come back looking for revenge for what has happened to him."

We were panic-stricken but we obeyed him. He instructed us to go to my grandfather's house, which was in a different section of the city. He and mother would join us later, he said. He had a reason why he did not leave with us: he wanted to alert the others who lived in our building to the situation. Mr. Schultz would most probably seek his revenge on them if he could not find us. When they finally left our apartment, my parents did not lock the door, so that it would seem they had just stepped out for a while.

We children were shocked beyond comprehension. Besides the horror of the situation, we were wounded emotionally by the actions of our supposed "friend" with whom we had shared so many hours. He had been like a member of our family. We could not understand how a person could change so fast, from one thing to its opposite.

But as time went on, we saw that it was not uncommon for gentile friends of Jews to become their foes and cooperate with the Nazis in carrying out the "final solution to the Jewish question." These turncoats were very good at rounding up Jews for work and pointing out to the Nazis Jews of means. For this service they were well rewarded by their German masters. They also informed the Gestapo of Jewish hiding places. Sometimes they hid Jews in exchange for possessions, and after they had extorted all the Jews had, betrayed them to the SS. In many instances, Jewish parents wanting to save their children entrusted them to gentile neighbors, giving the latter large sums of money and all their valuables. Then, soon after these parents were killed, the gentiles gave the children to the Gestapo to be killed in turn.

Mr. Schultz was not unique in his conduct toward the Jews. He was just one of many Polish gentiles who changed overnight, unleashing a restrained lifelong anti-Semitism.

The Nazis were very well aware of the deeply rooted hatred of the Poles toward the Jews. It was an essential element in the systematic and methodical extermination of the Jews. The Germans needed the collaboration of the natives of the country in which they established their treacherous and bestial death factories, and they found it among the Poles.

The Germans, planning to obliterate us completely, first clamped down on our city with harrowing bestiality. Jews were exposed to murder and assaults every hour of the day and night. My mother, being a physically weak person, suffered a heart attack when two SS soldiers burst into our apartment, made an "inspection," grabbed all our silver goblets, my mother's candelabrum, and my father's silver Chanukah lamp. Then one of them pulled my mother's wedding ring right off her finger, while the other beat my father. When my mother saw the latter point his rifle, she fainted. After the SS men departed, leaving the house in disarray, my father called a doctor, who had her admitted to a hospital.

The doctor was a German, and the hospital was in the far end of the city, where no Jews had ever lived even before the war. We were very much surprised to see that Dr. Milke treated my mother well—in complete contrast to the way she had just recently been treated by other Germans. Dr. Milke was also friendly to my father and to us children. Seeing that we were very frightened, he smiled at us and said we should not worry, he would take care of mother. When I asked him if I would be able to see my mother, he told me I could and said that I could even come to his house to find out about her condition.

The Germans were hunting Jews every day. They trapped them in the streets and sent them off to slave labor camps or used them for their sadistic amusement, beating them mercilessly and plucking or setting fire to their beards and sidelocks. Neither my father nor my brother would go out into the street since they wore beards and sidelocks. My

The Jews were used not only for labor and looting but also as objects of amusement, ridicule, and hate. A rabbi, in an open wagon, wrapped in a prayer shawl is carrying a sign saying, "We wanted the war."

younger sister being too small and fragile to take care of things outside the house, it fell upon me to become the family's sole provider and communicator between ourselves and the outside world. I was the only one able to visit my mother in the hospital.

When I was not with my mother, I worried constantly about her welfare. Although I knew that she couldn't stay home, I feared that something bad might happen to her in the hospital. In those days Jewish life had no value. And there she was the only Jewish woman amid hostile surroundings. Probably because my imagination overreacted with the fear I lived with during the day, I had terrible dreams about my mother at night. I was impatient for the sun to rise. I wanted to run to the hospital and convince myself that mother was alive, that no evil had hurt her.

Early in the morning my sister cooked a light soup for mother. Since it was a Christian hospital we knew that mother would not eat most of the foods there. As soon as the soup was ready I packed the pot in a basket and started out. I had to summon all my couage for this venture. It was hazardous for a Jew, even a girl, to show her face in the city.

The streets were almost deserted. Because of the terror the Nazis inflicted on us from the very start of their regime, Jews were reluctant to show themselves on the streets for fear of being shot, beaten or caught for hard labor—all of which often ended in death or permanent injury. Here or there I could see a woman or a child walking with hurried steps, as if anxious to erase the distance to her destination. Sometimes I saw a peasant woman, who had just come from her village, carrying a loaf of bread wrapped in a white cloth under her arm or in her basket. She was bringing the bread from the Aryan side of the city to sell it to a Jew. She knew that her merchandise was more valuable to the Jews than gold. They gladly exchanged their gold for what she was carrying. I smelled the fresh aroma of the bread and it made me feel hungry. It was almost a month since I had eaten a piece of bread. When bread became scarce, mother used potatoes and some kind of grain she acquired at the start of the war as a substitute. We ate what she cooked rather than stand in line a whole night in hope of buying bread. Now, when the peasant woman passed me with her loaf, my mouth started to water. I felt an overpowering desire to sink my teeth into that fresh crusty dough. But I was soon ashamed of my thoughts, and I tried to subdue my lust for food. I had more important things to think of. I had to reach the hospital as soon as possible. Maybe my mother was hungry and waiting for me to come.

I quickened my steps. I still had a long distance to go. Up till now I had seen an occasional person, but here the streets were completely deserted. The big apartment houses gave way to small one-family homes. None were Jewish homes. No Jews ever lived here. Some dogs were barking. My footfalls disturbed them. Some people were staring at me from behind closed shades. I walked with a secure step, but deep inside I was terrified. The emptiness and the silence of the streets frightened me.

I was also frightened by thoughts of what might happen to my mother in the hospital. Poison could be put in her food or she could be given a lethal injection. It would then be reported that she had died of natural causes. My heart started to palpitate as if it wanted to free itself from my imprisoning chest. More frightening thoughts raced through my mind. I imagined the worst. I began to run. When I was out of breath I stopped. I lifted my eyes and saw a three-story building. From my basket I took out a piece of paper with the address of the hospital written on it. I sighed with relief. This building was indeed the place where my mother was right now. I touched the towel which covered the little pot of soup, and was content to feel that it was still warm. With a heavy heart I entered the building.

My mother was very weak but not afraid. She told me that the nurse had compassion, that the other patients were indifferent to her. They were too occupied with their own illnesses to show any hostility. Seeing her very calm and hearing that she was well treated, I felt relaxed and relieved. From the hospital I went to the house of Dr. Milke. He told me that mother had had a slight heart attack, and that her heart was enlarged. He advised that, regardless of the unpredictable situation in the city, she stay in the hospital at least another week. He must have read my thoughts, for he again assured me that he himself would take good care of her. With a lighter heart and a more confident step, I started for home.

The week my mother stayed in the hospital was the longest in my life, for every day of it new decrees were published, singling out Jews as undesirable citizens. It was not that I didn't trust that hospital; it was rather that I realized my mother was the only "undesirable" person there. My fears for her well-being increased, because the terror in the city grew worse and worse with every passing day. The Jews lost all protection of the law. But at least they were together. Collectivity raised morale and gave the individual emotional support, while my mother was alone amidst enemies. As soon as the crisis of her illness was over, I was glad to take her home from the hospital, and only then could I breathe easier.

At that time a new decree came forth: all Jews were to wear a yellow armband. Disobedience to the decree was punishable by death. Its intention was clear: if Jews were easily distinguished from among other nationalities, they would be easier targets for the Germans. This decree was followed by another which declared that Jews were not to show their faces in non-Jewish sections of the city. Yet another decree forbade Jews to walk on Piotrokowska Street, the most popular, most busy, most luxurious, most Jewish street in Lodz. Jews who were prepared to pay for the privilege, however, could buy permits to walk on this street. Otherwise, if caught, they were sent away and never heard from again. One evening the Nazis burst into the most elegant cafe on Piotrokowska Street, when the place was full of diners and arrested half of the guests and shot the other half on the spot. These were the conditions we lived under for about three or four months—beyond the protection of the law, apart from other human society, separated from a normal economy, and from any possibility of existing as normal people.

After the yellow bands came the yellow star. We were ordered to wear a yellow star on the front and back of each garment when we went outside. Then, after restricting us from walking on most Jewish streets, the Germans listed the hours we could walk on permitted streets— between 8 a.m. and 5 p.m. Those who violated these edicts were sent away or summarily shot. Thousands of Jews, especially the young, ran away to other towns only to find out that the Nazis' arms were long. There was no eluding them. They reached all over Poland. Only those who escaped to the Russian side were safe for the time being.

Because the rumors that began in the beginning of December, 1939, that Lodz was to become *Judenrein*, free of Jews, did not subside, the Jews became very alarmed. Those with money fled to other towns, especially to Warsaw. But those who had meager means had to stay put. We were among this category. We had no money and nothing of value to exchange for money. The escape could be carried out only with the help of Poles or Germans, who required enormous bribes. They weren't interested in saving Jews but only in feathering their own nests.

On December 15, 1939, the Nazis decreed that all Jews would have to clear out of Lodz. At the beginning of February, 1940, they announced that a ghetto would be created for the Jews in the Baluty section, the poorest section of the city.

Never in my life can I forget our move to the ghetto. This unimaginable event stands out in my mind as vividly as if it happened only yesterday: mothers with crying children at their sides, some holding in their arms nursing babies, pushing a turned-over table, which served as a sled carrying all of the family's possessions. Old people carried their belongings tied on their backs. white-bearded elders clutched a bundle of books tied together with string under one arm and a bag with prayer shawl and phylacteries, the most precious possessions of the Jew, under the other.

The procession to the ghetto lasted many days. This terrible sight symbolized the misery and doom of our people. Nature too added to our

Pilsudskiego (Wschodnia) Street. The only street the Germans allowed us to use for the move to the ghetto. Rich and poor alike marched to Baluty carrying their possessions on their backs and in their hands.

anguish and conspired with our cruel enemy. The frost bit our faces and froze our breath; the violent wind tugged at shabby clothes and head coverings. Old people said that they could not remember such brutal weather. I remember that it was 25 degrees below zero.

Besides feeling helpless, I felt horrified, degraded and humiliated, thinking of what awaited us in the future. I wanted to run, but I felt caged. I wanted to die of the cold, but I had obligations to my family. I wanted to get rid of my life, but then who would take care of my mother.

I watched the procession and thought of how we might bring our belongings to the ghetto. This was actually less of a problem than how to get mother there. She had hardly recuperated from her heart attack. I stood on the street and watched other families move in confusion. The situation was hopeless. First of all, the distance was too far for her to walk and, secondly, the frost was too cruel for her to endure the journey. I was in a dilemma. To whom could I turn? Everyone was in the same position. Crying children, old and lame and sick were marching, blowing into their palms, knocking foot against foot, hitting the hardened snow with the soles of their shoes to keep their toes from freezing. Everyone needed help.

A thought flickered through my mind: I would try the *Linas Ha-Cholim*! The *Linas Ha-Cholim* was a health agency partially supported by the *Kehillah*, (the organized Jewish community). We had used them often, because my mother had always been a fragile person. I would go there and insist that they provide transportation for mother.

The office was humming with people who had come there to look for help. There were so many people that I had a hard time squeezing myself past the door. But once inside I decided I would not move until I got what I came for. Finally, I was able to present my case to one official, but he hardly seemed to listen. I repeated my request, but he told me that in view of the tragedy that had befallen all Jews of the city, he could not take care of my problem.

For a moment I was taken aback. Perhaps I was being too egotistical and selfish. There were so many sick, so many old, so many people in dire need of help. Why then should I be asking favors? But my instinct told me I was right. I was not asking anything for myself. I was asking help for my sick mother! I wiped away my tears of shame, straightened my back, and was ready to resume my quest.

The officials were running back and forth, in and out. The commotion was so great that one could hardly hear oneself speak. For a while I didn't approach anyone. I just studied the faces and attitudes of the *Linas Ha-cholim* representatives in dealing with people.

Behind a small window a young man was sitting and working. I noticed that he spent more time with people than the others did. A long line of people were waiting to speak to him. I got into that line. It moved very slowly. Each time when the line stopped moving the people near me startled to grumble. In contrast, the people who finished speaking to the man behind the window seemed to undergo a complete change of mood.

I knew that I was in the right place if I wanted to achieve my goal; however, I became annoyed when I looked at the clock ticking away the time. I knew that the young man would not sit in his place forever. Then, just as I got up to the window, the young man stuck his head out and announced that he was finished for the day. If he had hit me with a stone, he could not have hurt me more. I felt abandoned. My only hope was gone. The people in line behind me started to shout and scream, but the young man apologized and left. One by one the other officials left, and so did the people who had come to speak with them. The people were disappointed and bitter. I did not leave. I told myself it would be better to sleep in the street than go home without accomplishing what I had set out to do.

When the hall was quite empty and no one there, I began opening doors. The doors were unlocked but the rooms behind them were empty. I had opened maybe eight doors when, in a corner, in what looked like an exit, I found yet another door and opened it. I saw a woman in her thirties sitting at a table. The room was the size of a closet. She looked at me surprised, but asked me to come in. When I did so, she pulled a chair from behind her desk and told me to sit down.

I was not prepared for kindness at that moment, and all the sobs that were locked in my throat welled up and tears filled my eyes. The woman let me cry. When I finished crying I told the woman my problem. She listened to me without interruption, then asked me to wait. After about ten minutes, an old man walked in. She told him my story. He looked at me, turned to her and gave her instructions to make a telephone call and left the room. After she put away the telephone, she turned to me and said that a *dorozhka*, a horse-drawn carriage, would be waiting for me outside in the street. I wanted to say something to thank her, but the words stuck in my throat and I could not force them out. The woman looked at me with her big black eyes and said she understood. The old man was Chaim Rumkowski, *Der Alteste der Juden* and the lady's future husband.

There was no happier person in the world than I when I felt the small step of the carriage underneath my foot. And when I rode into our courtyard my parents could hardly believe what they saw. There was still a whole hour to sundown. But we had to rush because of the curfew. In haste I grabbed the two down quilts. One I put on the seat to protect mother from the cold underneath her and the other I wrapped completely around her. I put some of her essential things in the carriage bedding, some linen. I climbed onto the carriage step and gave the driver my uncle's address in the section of the city where the ghetto had been created.

Whenever I recall my trip to the ghetto, a great anger wells up in me. I can still feel the degrading pain I felt when I joined that procession. Thousands of Jews were walking with some of their possessions on their back, carrying what they could carry in their hands, and sliding still others along the frozen street. The only street the Germans allowed us to use in our relocation was packed with people, rich and poor, who had had to leave the homes where they had lived all their lives. Very few of them had a place to go to. They were simply running away from death. But death would reach them eventually.

Even so, they had to move aside to make space whenever a vehicle had to go by. Jews going to the ghetto were not allowed to use the sidewalks. Standing on the step of the slowly-moving carriage, I felt worse than if I had been part of the crowd on foot. I felt degraded and subdued. I felt such an anger inside me that I wanted to destroy everything around me. My anger grew out of my own powerlessness and the powerlessness of all the people around me. I wondered if they felt the same way I did. Was there really nothing left for us but blindly following orders? My blood was boiling when we finally reached my uncle's home.

My father's youngest brother, Uncle Fishel, had seven children. The oldest, Mordechai, was fourteen years old and the youngest was an infant girl born in November, 1939. They were our only relatives who lived in the section which was proclaimed the ghetto. At the end of December, 1939, the Gestapo, unexpectedly and in the darkness of night, entered the neighborhood where my uncle lived and dragged many

Jews from their beds and deported them. None of the deportees ever returned. Among them were my uncle Fishel and five of his seven children.

My aunt Gittel was ill, at that time bedridden with a blood clot in her leg following the delivery of her latest child. When the Gestapo took away my uncle and five of his children, leaving her, the infant and Mordechai in the apartment, they sealed the door from the outside. For five days my aunt and the two children were locked in. On the sixth day Mordechai managed to break open the door. I remember when he came running to us and told us what had happened. All we could do was give him some food. I went with him to other relatives, and they, too, provided him with food.

When the Germans forced us out of our home, the only place we could think of to go was my uncle's apartment.

When we arrived there it was already evening. We found many of our relatives there. That evening, including my immediate family, twenty-seven people were present. The apartment consisted of an average size bedroom, an average kitchen, and a walk-in closet with a small window which served as a children's room. We were welcomed, but everyone in the family worried about my mother's health.

Arrangements for the night were such that most of us slept on the floor. But my mother was given the table to sleep on, the best place in these circumstances. My sister and I slept under the table. There was almost no air to breathe. In addition to the congestion of people, the contours of the apartment added to its stuffiness. In the bedroom the ceiling sloped on one side, and in the children's room the slope was so steep that a person five foot tall could not stand up straight. Only a small child could be comfortable there.

The restlessness of my mother woke me up in the middle of the night. She was short of breath. Not knowing what to do I forced open the window to let in air. But with the wind a sheet of snow swept in from the roof across the way. Now the room had air but it also had a lot of wind, snow, and cold. And because of wind and snow I couldn't close the window. I started to freeze. I was afraid that mother would catch pneumonia. She was right in front of the open window. I saw no way out of the situation. What could I do? I looked for things to cover mother with. I didn't care to whom they belonged. I pulled out whatever came to my hand and laid it on mother. She started to cough, first softly, then spasmodically. I prayed to G-d for the night to end, though I didn't know what I could do in the morning. I just knew that this night was frightening me.

It frightened me because of my mother's condition, and not because of my or my family's discomfort. I knew that there were families who didn't have even a crowded lodging for the night. People who didn't have relatives or money to pay for a place to sleep had nowhere to turn. Many of these unfortunates slept on staircases and in gateways of houses. If not for my mother's health, I would consider myself lucky. But I was in anguish about her. Where would I get a doctor for her? After this night she would need medical help again.

Early next morning I woke up my brother. I told him to wrap his face in a shawl, so that his beard and sidelocks would not show. He wouldn't look suspicious because the frost was biting. I said we must go out together to look for an apartment. Another night like this would cause my mother another heart attack. We got some money from my father and then went from house to house asking if there was any apartment available. None was. My brother reasoned that we had no chance to find a decent place in the heart of the ghetto, but if we ventured closer to the Aryan side, we might do better, since few Jews wanted to risk being exposed to our enemies. In our case we had to take that risk. We had to do what was good for mother. My brother had a logical mind. He was almost always right. He was right this time, too.

The sun slowly slanted up from the horizon, and the snow stopped falling, but the frost was unrelenting. With hasty steps we walked toward the outskirts of the town. When we were out of the Jewish section I became a little uneasy. My brother noticed it and asked me: "What's wrong?"

"Can't you see what's happening to us, Benjamin? The Nazis hunt us down like animals. Our lives and our future turn to dust and ashes in front of our very eyes. It seems that we are doomed. Are we just to accept our fate and thank G-d for it?" I said in anger.

"Did you ever read any Jewish history books?" he asked me. "Do you know that our ghetto happens not to be the first one. There were ghettos before. From time immemorial the Jews suffered persecution. We are but one link in the long chain of our history of suffering. The only difference is that now we ourselves happen to be a link in that chain. As long as you, my dear sister, could read about what happened to our people, you could tolerate the pain others suffered; however, when you yourself are involved in suffering, you're ready to lose yourself, and with that your sense of obligation as one of our people. Are you ready to doubt your faith because you suffer? I think that now is the time to learn to be strong, to know how to act in the face of our suffering and to understand the meaning of our suffering.''

I didn't interrupt him. He made me realize that our enemies had always wanted to crush us and that now was no different. The Nazis' aim he said was to destroy our faith, but we must do everything to be sure they did not succeed. I felt ashamed, and my boiling anger cooled. He was right. Still, I sensed that I was not as strong as he was. I envied him.

Immersed in our discussion, we did not realize we had reached a sparsely populated area. Here small houses with little gardens and tall trees dotted the landscape. We arrived at a fenced-in garden, with a broad branched tree and a wooden bench. Fastened to the fence was another bench. A bench under a tree in a garden full of flowers is exactly what mother needs now, I thought, but my brother said it aloud, and he pulled the wire bell at the low wooden gate. A gentile woman came out and asked what we wanted. She saw that we were Jews, and we knew that she would soon leave her house for a finer house or a spacious apartment outside the ghetto.

When we asked her if we could rent a part of her house, she said we could but that she wanted two hundred zlotys. It is a cruel trick, I thought to myself. Why should she ask us for so much money, when she knows as well as we do that she will get a luxurious Jewish apartment for no money at all.

As I opened my mouth to say something, my brother stopped me, and turning to the woman asked: ''Would you move out today if we gave you the money?'' She looked at him and said: ''Yes.'' Observing my brother reaching in his pocket for the money, she added: ''If you pay me the full amount now, I'll go now and I will leave you two iron beds besides.''

Benjamin gave her the money and she led us into the house. We came into a room, ten by fourteen feet. There were two windows looking down into the garden. The room was completely empty except for the two iron beds, both standing against the long wall of the room. The fact that the room was otherwise unfurnished made me think that she had already moved out before we came and only waited for an opportunity to press money from the Jews. She showed us that the mattresses had fresh straw. Then she put the money in her pocket and gave us the key. I looked at my brother telling him with my eyes that I thought the woman had taken advantage of us. Why had he been so fast to give her the money? Why hadn't he bargained with her? He put the key in his pocket, and wished her all the best, and we left the house.

On the way home I reproached him for being too hasty. "It is irrelevant if this woman took advantage of us or not," he answered. "What counts is that we got exactly what we wanted and needed for mother. However, the more important thing is to remember, especially now, when we are approaching a new phase in our lives, that we have to learn how to act, even with a gentile woman. She is also being resettled. Sometimes the grandest apartment cannot take the place of a poor home when the home is taken away by force. If we will not stand on guard, and see the importance of even the smallest things that happen to others, we will be crushed, morally, very fast."

My brother was four years older than I. Until he was Bar-Mitzva at thirteen, we used to play together, take walks together, and enjoy things together. But then he started to change. He became very serious in his studies of the Talmud and had very little time to "waste" with me and my sister. I, on the other hand, became busy with school and friends. Each of us turned to his or her own personal interests. Now I felt a real closeness to him again, the kind of closeness which gives meaning to life. I felt that his spiritual strength could be my moral support at a time of need. What I learned that day was that Benjamin was more prepared than I was to cope with the rigors of our new life. At a time when I felt angry at the whole world, he showed calm and wisdom. He had answers while I just agitated myself with questions.

The purpose of the ghetto was to crush the Jews spiritually. My brother had tried to awaken in me the spiritual strength I needed for the ordeal that lay ahead.

4. The Ghetto

The first phase of the Final Solution was to concentrate all Jews in ghettos. The Nazis believed that by subjecting their victims to inhuman conditions they would cause them to commit suicide en masse or kill each other by fighting for their survival, and that those who survived would die from starvation and disease. The first of these notions proved very disappointing to the Germans, though the second proved to be all too true.

Nevertheless, in pursuit of their objective to destroy their victims, the Nazis turned life in the ghetto into one tremendous, long nightmare. Our nights and days were filled with misery, privation, disease, and hunger. The pattern of existence the Nazis designed for us had the purpose of bringing a speedy death to the Jewish community. But although many thousands died daily, the murderers were not satisfied with the pace at which our people died.

The ghettos were supposed to function as an instrument of psychological and spiritual as well as of physical destruction. The Jews were to be crushed spiritually even before the final liquidation of the inmates of the ghettos. This was a very carefully designed plan for the first phase of the Final Solution.

The Germans also depended on a high suicide rate among the ghetto prisoners. Their logic was that by isolating us from the rest of the population of the city, by putting us behind wire fences and high walls in restricted quarters under outrageous conditions, and also subjecting us to starvation and savage brutality, we would be made happy to part with our lives. However, they misjudged the Jewish spirit. For when we were faced with total annihilation, we looked for avenues of resistance. Even under the shadow of extermination we clung to life, totally contradicting our enemy's line of reasoning. Isolated from the outside world, the Jews turned inward. They found sustenance in their tradition and held on to their heritage, more so than before the war. The leaders of the ghetto decided that this was the time to go back to our Jewish origins. They realized that assimilation and adaptation to other cultures had proved fruitless. In the normal prewar conditions the Jewish intelligentsia shunned their roots and tried to identify themselves with the cultural world of the non-Jews. Our "president," Rumkowski, decided to establish a curriculum in the schools of the ghetto, where students would learn what it meant to be a Jew. This transformation took place in light of the realization that embracing foreign cultures had not lessened the alienation of the Jewish people. They had been deceived by the world which they tried so hard to emulate. Now, in the ghetto they sought a new sense of identity and found it in the link which they had tried to sever. In Judaism they realized continuity, a cohesive bonding through all the generations.

As soon as the ghetto was stabilized, elementary schools and high schools were established emphasizing Yiddish as the prime language in the curriculum. Jewish history, the Bible, and the prophets were studied as major subjects. The assimilated youth of our ghetto found a new direction and a new outlook on life as Jews. Yiddish literature, Yiddish language, and Yiddish history—subjects which were neglected before the war—were seized on with great zest by these young people. They also adopted the idea of Zionism, which flourished in the ghetto. The concept of *Shivat Zion*, return to Zion, to the land of our forefathers, was never so well appreciated and understood as it was in the destructive circumstances of ghetto life. Although the chances were very remote that one day they would reach the dreamed-of land, it was of urgent importance for the youth to live with hope that a future for them was still possible.

The dream of another, better life, in the most horrible conditions and in such extreme desolation, was of paramount importance to self-preservation, and it became a potent weapon in the struggle for survival. It was a kind of resistance to the Nazi oppression.

Now, if the ghetto was created with the aim of destroying the will-power of the victims to struggle and live, then the determination of the inmates to remain alive at all costs was another way of expressing resistance. When the ghetto became a reality, the Jews mobilized all their resources to establish a cultural life in this hell to which they were consigned. Every organization formed literary groups for reading, writing, and lectures. New books were written; new plays and new music were composed, and theatre and an orchestra were established to perform them! Underground religious groups were formed for prayer and the study of Torah. In secret they formed *minyans,* and three times a day people met and united in prayer, expressing faith in the Almighty. These activities were a proof that the Jewish spirit did not crumble under the iron boot of the Nazi oppressor. We were determined to live at all costs.

Once the ghetto had been closed, it became clear to all inside that gigantic prison the ghetto was, that it would become a reflection of Nazi Germany, with Rumkowski, the Jewish dictator, a tool and puppet of the Nazis. He became another instrument of the destruction of the Jews. He created his own theories and slogans. One of his more frequent slogans was: "Work is our passport to life." When he established a relief list of the unemployed (which meant 85% of the ghetto population), he should have aroused a degree of suspicion. But most people did not speculate on the list, for they had no other source of income. They accepted this financial aid, not realizing that they would eventually have to pay for it. When the Nazis demanded the first large transport of ghetto inmates for deportation, Rumkowski had a ready roster and a convenient excuse for deporting "unproductive" people.

In those days the only media of communication in the ghetto were official gatherings and posters pasted on walls and poles. Later there were newspapers. In the fall of 1940, before the *Ghetto Zeitung* (the Ghetto Newspaper) was printed, posters appeared on all poles and walls announcing Rumkowski's decision that all unemployed would get financial aid from the ghetto administration. The payments were to be distributed the first day of every month by special clerks. These posters were signed and sealed by Rumkowski himself.

I was sixteen years old. I did not have the experience older people had. Yet, I felt that I should warn everybody not to take the money Rumkowski offered. I also knew that nobody would listen to me and rightly so. Who was I to know? I had no special information. I just had a hunch, and this was not enough to convince people. Even now, when my memories turn to those fateful days, I can still feel the fearful suspicion Rumkowski's "generosity" evoked in me. I did not trust him. I felt that he was trying to entrap us.

My parents were already calculating what we could buy with the money we would get every month. I did not agree with their idea of blindly accepting Rumkowski's welfare. I said that we had to look into the reason why he wanted to support the unemployed, while all his other efforts were directed toward proving to the Germans the productiveness of the ghetto inmates. He used to lecture us to the effect that as long as we were productive we would be needed, that not only the feeding of the ghetto, but its sheer existence depended on our productivity. Even then it was already clear that the Nazis' aim was to exterminate the Jews. Their cruelty toward the Jews proved it. But the Germans might be in no hurry to destroy us as long as they could use us. Still, I could not see how their naked brutality accorded with a concern for the unemployed. Why didn't my parents and many other thousands of people see the situation the way I saw it? The truth of the matter is that they did, but they had no other choice. The only alternative was starvation.

I do not know what prompted me to act the way I did, to act so strongly only because of an intuition. But I begged my parents not to accept the money of the *zasilek*. When they asked me how I thought they could buy the allotted ration of food, I said that I would look for work and earn it. I had no idea how I might carry out my plan. I didn't even know how to start. My compulsion to reject the *zasilek* was a reaction to an inner voice which told me that the *zasilek* was prelude to a great tragedy. Yet I wasn't too sure of myself; my self-confidence was mixed with fear and doubts. What if I did not succeed in finding a job, and then it was too late to register for the welfare? But the impossible happened in the following manner.

I did not know if it was excitement or fear that did not let me sleep that night. I felt a terrible burden on my shoulders. I was thinking that I might regret my hasty decision. What if I coudn't find work? What if I found work which I wouldn't be able to perform? Had I made a mistake by being overconfident in myself? These questions tortured me greatly through much of the night. Early next morning I left the house without telling anyone where I was heading The fact was I didn't know myself. I needed to think in the open air.

A cheering sun met me on the road to Marishin. Why did I choose the road leading to Marishin? I do not know. Perhaps it was predestined. At that moment I felt I needed to breathe. I needed the free sky and clear air. I felt so tight inside myself that instinctively I was drawn to where nature was still to be found. Marishin was the only place in the ghetto where there were real trees and live flowers, where the air was filled with the fragrance of growing things.

My lungs expanded as they took in the fresh early spring air. What a sight presented itself to my eyes as I continued my walk. Low bushes with tiny green tomatoes; radish beds with new cabbage and carrot plants nearby them; young cucumber vines springing from the dark, wet soil. But when my eyes found the bed of proud-looking green scallions, I was smitten. How erect and majestic they stood, the gentle wind caressing their thin stalks. This was the first time since the ghetto had been established that I had seen so much of nature in one place. To whom could it all belong?

Suddenly I felt hands reach under my two arms, and I was lifted aloft. I was surprised to see Lubcia, my best friend, and her older sister, Surcia.

"Let's take her with us, Lubcia," Surcia said.

"Where to?" I asked.

"We will tell you while walking," Lubcia answered.

"Where are you two rushing to this early hour of the morning?" I asked in astonishment, after catching my breath. We were literally running.

"We're going to work, and we are late. We're almost there. You can walk home from there." Surcia knew that once Lubcia and I started to talk, we would never finish. To prevent this, she dragged me along.

We stopped at a shack full of work clothes and garden tools. In a hurry, they changed into some of the clothes. They seemed to have completely forgotten me. They grabbed their tools and were about to run out of the shack to their jobs when I suddenly burst into sobs. I couldn't hold back my tears. Surcia thought that she might have offended me, but when I told here the real reason for my crying, she asked me to wait while she spoke to her boss, who happened to also be her friend. Ten minutes later I was standing in the office of a tall young man, who handed me a working suit and a pair of garden tools. I had a job! A real job! I could not believe it! I had to pinch myself to be sure I was not dreaming. There wasn't a happier person in the world at that moment than I. And there were no sweeter blisters on anyone's hands than on mine after I finished my first day of work. And there was no back that hurt with such pleasure as mine did that first day of my first job.

It took less than one year for the Germans to demand the first transport of Jews for resettlement purposes. Many thousands of inmates of the ghetto, drawn from the list of *zasilek*, fed the pits, the flames, and the crude gas chambers with their innocent lives. *Zasilek* had been a trap, but when the people realized it, it was already too late. The first "list" took effect in the winter of 1941-1942. Because it was the first, most of us didn't understand the true meaning of it. It was explained to us that the Jews who left would be resettled in a new area where there was employment. This was the time when we were still naive. We believed what we were told. The truth was that all the people on the list were deported to Chelmno.

I had seldom heard of Chelmno before the war. It was never mentioned in my geography classes in school. None of my friends or relatives had lived there. And I had never heard my parents discuss anything associated with Chelmno, which was just one of many sleepy, little towns in the flat-lands of Poland. But now there is so much to be said about this place that not to speak out, not to focus on the issue of Chelmno, would be an almost inexcusable crime, because Chelmno is peopled with ghosts, with the souls of a great part of our people of Lodz. It conceals in its fertile earth the best of our young and old, of our parents and our children. It is a cemetery containing the ashes of a great part of our nation, for here the Germans established a special extermination camp for Jews.

The monstrous death factory in Chelmno was opened on December 8, 1941, and it was in operation until January 1945. About 351,000 Jews from Lodz and surrounding areas were murdered there.

Two witnesses, Walenti Oshatowicz, commandant of the Chelmno fire department, and the mayor of the town, Jan Henriewicz, tell the story of this extermination camp.

German gendarmes, assisted by SS men, rounded up 1,500 Jews in Lenczitz and 800 Jews in Podembice, herded them to Chelmno, and locked them up in a church for three days and three nights. The crowding was terrible. There was no place to sit down. A woman gave birth to a baby while standing; she died of pain and the baby died soon after. Because of lack of air, the prisoners became violent and broke windows. Many tried to escape, were caught and tortured to death. The remainder were brought to a nearby woods and ordered to dig pits. They did not know that they were digging their own graves. When the pits were dug, they were forced to lie one next to the other, face down. All were shot in the back of the head by machine guns.

From January, 1942, onward, Jews who had been deported from Ghetto Lodz began to arrive in Chelmno. The first transport consisted of 750 families, about 3,000 men and women of all ages, the old as well as newborn babies. Some of them were ill and some were well, but all of them met the same fate.

The victims were not told where they were being taken or why. But the Germans planted a rumor among them that in Chelmno a Jewish community was being established for all the Jews of Poland. The truth of Chelmno, however, was that all Jews taken there disappeared. To deceive the victims till the last minute of their lives suited the goal of the Germans. They wanted no disturbances in their work. German efficiency and punctuality required order. The truth would have caused resistance, disturbed their order, so they filled the air with lies.

They spread another rumor that the Jews were being confined in a prince's castle in Chelmno, from which they would be taken in groups to neighboring places where work was available. The truth, however, was that they were herded into the woods and murdered.

New arrivals were first taken to the Chelmno Church. There they would lay down their belongings and be brought to the castle. The castle was a one-story remnant of a larger structure which was wrecked during the First World War. On its walls, in large letters, was painted "Bath Institution."

When the Jews arrived at the church, they would be met by Gestapo agents both in uniform and civilian clothes, and a large number of police. Besides the Jews, the Gestapo, and police, there were never any others present. No two transports were ever allowed to meet. In the beginning, when the groups of Jews arrived, they were treated courteously, even kindly. They were helped in getting down from the trucks they had come in. The Nazis used these tactics to disarm them.

An elderly German in civilian clothes particularly aroused their confidence. He had a soft gentle voice, and when he led the Jews into a large, well heated room lined with steps in the castle, they thought they had been taken to a public bath. From here they were escorted through an underground corridor, at the end of which was a ramp-like structure. This opened on a number of cellars. In one of these cellars, the kindly old German addressed the new arrivals. He told them that the entire transport was about to be sent to a ghetto in a nearby community. There the men would be employed in factories, the women would get jobs as housekeepers, and the children would be sent to schools. But before going to the ghetto all of them had to take a bath and submit to disinfection of themselves and their clothes. They would have to disrobe and surrender their documents, valuables, and money to prevent their being damaged.

When the speech ended, the entire group was led naked through a bitterly cold hallway back to the ramp. Once there, the situation changed completely. With whips and gun butts the Jews were driven into an execution vehicle. The victims experienced a terrible despair and fear. Some started to pray loudly, weeping and moaning, realizing that they had been brutally deceived and were caught in a net from which there was no escape.

There is the additional eyewitness account by a Mr. Mieszeczak, who lived near the prince's palace. In an article in the Polish newspaper *Nove Zycie*, (New Life), dated January 10, 1945, he describes the satanic procedures of the Germans in this death factory, noting that one of the trucks used for suffocating the Jews was still to be found in the nearby town of Kola.

A hundred people were forced into one truck. The rear doors were locked and sealed so that no air whatsoever could get in. After ten or fifteen minutes the people started to cough and gasp. Then the cries and moans died down. The walls of the truck were lined with tin and the floor was lined with ladders, under which were pipe openings, approximately 15 centimeters in diameter covered with sieve wire. There pipes were part of a gas mechanism at the front of the truck and controlled by the driver. When the victims were all sealed up inside, the truck would be driven some kilometers to the woods of Ziurkow, about two hundred steps from the road. There it was encircled by police armed with machine guns. Gathered beside a big dugout were about thirty SS men and fifty Jewish grave diggers naked but for the shirts they wore. The truck would continue moving and halt about a hundred yards from the prepared grave. Then the driver would turn on the gas apparatus and leave the truck. His function was a double one—chauffeur and executioner.

From the truck one could hear stifled cries, howls, and poundings on the walls. After about fifteen minutes all became quiet. When the chauffeur had made sure that all the victims were dead, he would drive the truck nearer to the grave and open its doors. A terrible stinging odor of gas would fill the air. After a while some of the grave diggers would remove the bodies from the truck, while others would hurl the corpses into the grave, and still others would place them in position as ordered by the SS men. Two German civilians would examine every corpse, so as to get the last possessions from the dead. With pliers they would extract gold teeth. They would rip rings off fingers and make sure that no hidden valuables were in the sex organs of the women. The desecrated corpses would then be lined up in straight rows in the grave. The head of one victim would be placed on top of the feet of another, and the empty places would be filled with small children. After a layer of earth was thrown over them, another tier of corpses would be placed in the grave. When transports from the Lodz Ghetto began arriving, the grave diggers were working until late at night. They had to do their work in the glare of floodlights. Oftentimes, the diggers were compelled to bury their own murdered loved ones.

The eight grave diggers inside the dugout were not permitted to leave their posts. They were beaten mercilessly while they worked. In the evening, these eight would be commanded to lie down in the grave, facing the corpses, and an SS man would riddle their brains with machine gun bullets. The other grave diggers would be confined to cellars of the castle under triple lock. In the morning an SS officer would order them out of the cellars and, after counting them numerous times, into the truck, which took them to the place of execution. The grave diggers were under surveillance from the moment they left the cellars in the morning until they returned to them at night. Any sign of fatigue or protest was likely to result in death.

On numerous occasions, the grave diggers smashed windows and threw letters out the chimney to inform the outside world of what was happening in Chelmno. Three grave diggers actually succeeded in escaping.

No matter how methodically and efficiently the death factory in Chelmno operated, the Nazis were not satisfied. There were complaints that the dead bodies were contaminating the air. A new way had to be found for disposing of bodies, and that, eventually, was burning. Primitive crematoriums were built, each using two long iron rails as grids. On top of the rails were put a layer of wood and a layer of bodies, layer upon layer. The benzene was poured over the bodies and wood and ignited. The bones of the bodies which were not burned to ashes were ground up in huge grinders. Many large parts of human bones were found in the fields after the war. The ashes were used to fertilize the earth and for other purposes.

The clothes of the victims were placed in a church in Dembia, which had been converted to a warehouse for victims' clothing. Jews worked at sorting these clothes. They themselves had been brought from the surrounding areas to Chelmno to be exterminated. But before they were gassed in the trucks they were put to work. Heavy chains were put on their feet so that they could not run away. After sorting, these clothes were shipped to Ghetto Lodz.

All churches of the Chelmno area became part of the extermination camp for Jews. On the walls of these churches the victims engraved their names, dates of deportation, and notes. "Today's transport of seven hundred Jews was here." "Yesterday a group of nine hundred people were here from Lodz." Some inscriptions tell where the victims were supposed to be taken, naming a new ghetto where they would be working and producing for the Germans. From these inscriptions it is clear that until their final moments, the Jews sustained hope and illusion, so great was the deception the Germans perpetrated.

Forty-five Jewish specialists worked in a tailoring shop. The night of January 16-17 1945, before the Russians entered Chelmno, these Jews were prepared for execution. First the SS men locked them in the shop; then they led them out in small groups. One of the prisoners threw himself with a knife on an SS man. For his temerity the rest were punished. They were returned to the shop again. The SS set the building on fire. All those inside perished that night. There are no survivors of Chelmno, the first primitive death factory in Poland. More than one million Jews died there. *haShem yikom damam!* God avenge their blood!

• • •

The frost was terrible that winter and there was no fuel with which to heat the one room we lived in. We did not get any wood or charcoal rations. We ghetto inmates chopped up and burned our wooden closets, cabinets, beds, and chairs. Later, we stole wood from fences, and houses, and sheds in order to have fuel. In one instance, the tenants of a house got up one morning only to find that the stairs had vanished during the night, along with the handrail and banister.

We lived in a wooden house. It was a two-story building, with six tenants. We and two other tenants lived in the second story. Above us was an attic. It was nice and clean. The floor was made of smooth and long wood boards. My sister and I used to play games there when we were hungry and there was no food in the house.

Once my sister and I discovered a loose panel. It was there for decorative purposes. That day the frost was very biting. We took the panel down to our apartment and fed our stove. The warmth made us feel very good, though we were not happy to have participated in an act of stealing. Days and weeks went by and the cold continued. The winter was long and the frost was unyielding. The walls of our room were covered with ice, and there was no fuel ration in prospect.

My mother fell ill. She developed a fever. We did not have anything to use to heat her some water. We had to choose between preserving my mother's health and our code of morality. We chose the former. From time to time we went up to the attic and removed a few boards to warm up the room and cook whatever food we happened to have. It did not take long before we discovered that we were not the only ones who were dismantling the attic. Often in the middle of the night we could hear someone ripping up boards and carrying them down the attic ladder. The real problems began when the snow started to melt and water leaked into our apartment. Later on, in the spring, we suffered terribly from the rain, too: the floor in our room became one big puddle. The following winter we had to start ripping out our own floor. We ripped out the board from above our heads. For the sake of the truth, I have to confess that we never tore even one board from the attic which was not above our heads.

Because the frost was unrelenting, stealing wood became an epidemic. When people were caught stealing wood they were sentenced to many months of imprisonment at hard labor. These sentences were often a prelude to deportation, which was equivalent to death.

One frosty day when my sister came back from work, she was approached by two Jewish policemen who asked for her identification. When she complied with their wishes she was arrested, and taken to the police station. She was brought up before two officials with whips in their hands threatening to beat her if she would not confess that she went to Mr. Bilander to get part of the wood he stole the night before.

My sister became confused and very frightened. It was the first time she had been confronted by police accusing her of a crime she did not commit. It was the first time she had been in a police station. She was panic stricken. She was so frightened that she could not talk. One policeman with a long rubber truncheon threatened to use it on her if she did not confess immediately.

Wanting to be done with the matter, she said, "Yes." The same policeman told her to sign a statement which he had prepared. After she had signed, he read her the statement, which said that her father had sent her to Mr. Bilander to get part of the wood he and her father had stolen during that night. After this she was released from the precinct.

On the way home she realized that she had made an injurious statement about her own father. At the police station she had been unable to think. She had just wanted to get out of that terrible place. The truth was that she had gone against her own father, by telling the truth, because she did go to Mr. Bilander for a few pieces of wood. She did not know that Mr. Bilander had made a statement at the police station that my father had sent her for a "part" of the wood which he, Bilander, had stolen from our fence. She knew Bilander because he used to rent us a bungalow in the country for the summer. But it was only now she realized that he had implicated my father in the crime he had committed the night before.

When she came back from the police station she found all our neighbors waiting for her. They wanted to know what had happened to her there. From them she also found out that father had been arrested earlier in the day. Only now did she comprehend the full gravity of the situation.

On the previous night, as on all his other nights in the ghetto, father went up to visit a friend who lived across the courtyard. Together with three other neighbors, they studied the Talmud every night. It was a very windy night and it started to snow. As always when the study session was over, father ran home, straight to bed. We were already sleeping. A few minutes later there was a knock at our door. My sister went to open it. There in the doorway stood Mr. Bilander. My sister told him that father was already asleep, but he begged her to let him in. He would just be a moment.

Mr. Bilander knelt at father's bed, pleading with him not to tell what he had seen. Father started to laugh. He thought that Bilander was making a joke. He did not understand what this man was up to. Father was tired, hungry, and cold, and wanted to go back to his sleep. He told Mr. Bilander: "Sir, I do not know what you are talking about. I did not see anything. I just came home. I am sure that you need your sleep just as I need mine. Go home and rest. It is late." Bilander, however, did not go home right away. He insisted that father send his daughter to him in the morning. He wanted to give father a few pieces of wood.

My sister heard the whole conversation. Early in the morning she got up and told father that she was going to Bilander before going to work, to get the wood. Father agreed. Going home with such a treasure, she felt very happy that it would be she who brought home some fuel, so that she might be able to cook something warm for mother.

It turned out that during the night Bilander came to our backyard and stole the small wooden gate of our fence. A short time before that our "President," Rumkowski, had decreed that stealing wood, especially from public property, like garbage recepticals, latrines, and fences, would be considered a crime resulting in a prolonged prison sentence. He made the supers of the houses responsible for guarding such public property. When Bilander tore away our gate, our super, hearing a noise, came to his window and watched what Bilander was doing. In the morning he reported him to the police. He knew Bilander because he lived in our neighborhood. Bilander was arrested that same morning.

Mr. Bilander had not been aware that someone had seen him dismantle our gate, besides father, who had happened to walk by when he was ready to leave with his loot. Because he was afraid that father might report him to the police, he had promised him the wood. When he was arrested, he conjectured that father had reported him. So when he was interrogated he claimed that he had had an accomplice in his crime, and he gave father's name. He also told the police that he gave part of his loot to my sister. My sister's testimony, although forced out, fit this picture perfectly. She could not forgive herself for what she had done. She said that if father was found guilty she would commit suicide.

Until the trial, father was imprisoned. My sister could not sleep nights.

Once when one of our neighbors, a young man named Oscar, asked about father's trial she confessed what was on her mind, saying that if father were found guilty she would not be able to go on living. Oscar was a bright man; he had been a law student until the war broke out. He made my sister go over her testimony at the police station, word for word, time after time, until she became weary. But he made her understand that there was a big difference between her claim that she had gone to Bilander for a few pieces of wood which he had promised and the statement she had been made to sign that she went to him for a part of the wood which he and her father had stolen together.

For the trial we hired a lawyer, Mrs. Cederbaum. She was the daughter of my father's friend. She did not charge us for appearing in court. The three friends with whom my father had studied that night came to testify. Our super, our second prime witness, was there on time.

Mr. Bilander also hired a lawyer. He also brought witnesses. First my mother was called to the stand. She declared what she knew: that Mr. Bilander had begged her husband not to say anything. She had also heard Bilander tell my father to send his daughter for some wood. My brother and I testified the same thing. The prime witness on our side was my sister. She was the one who had picked up the wood, and on her testimony hinged the outcome of the trial. Just as she was confused at the police station, so in the court she was composed, stating that she had gone to Bilander for "pieces of wood" rather then "part of the wood," as she had attested to the police. Then the witnesses for our side were called to the stand. Their testimony as to the time they had been with father fitted with the time the super had told the police the crime took place. Every piece of evidence given by our witnesses dovetailed perfectly with every other piece of evidence. Quite the opposite was the case with Bilander's witnesses. They were false witnesses. They were afraid to claim that they were on the spot while Bilander was *not* stealing our gate. How could they explain being in the middle of the night in a strange courtyard? They could testify only to Bilander's good character.

At the trial Bilander was confused and surprised. First, he did not know that there was someone who had actually seen him stealing the gate. And secondly, he was surprised to discover that father had not been the one to report him. He realized his mistake, but too late.

Why had he been so sure of himself? Because he was released after interrogation while father was not.

Father walked away from the court a free man, while Mr. Bilander was put in jail. What happened to him I do not know.

This episode illustrates our miserable life in the ghetto. Mr. Bilander was not a criminal. He stole the wood because he wanted to warm his home or boil a little warm water. Even if it was true, as some people said, that he sold the wood, was the crime so great that he should have been deported and never heard of again? If he stole the wood to sell it, he did not do so to buy luxuries, but ony a piece of bread for his children or possibly for himself. Is this such a terrible crime? Yes, in the ghetto it was. Because we were put in the ghetto to die fast, and acts like Mr. Bilander's postponed the dying. So what he had done was a terrible crime in a world of madness and cruelty. It did not fit in with the program of the Germans, the destruction of the Jews at the highest possible speed.

In the gray winter days and snow white winter nights of late 1941 a heavy despair and dark foreboding spread over the ghetto. The new year started with a new deportation on January 15 which lasted till January 29, 1942. In those two weeks more than ten thousand people were deported to Chelmno. They never returned. Ghetto Lodz became a hell on earth. People were dragged from their beds, from the streets, and from the shops. Families were torn apart. Children became orphans and parents became childless overnight. It was a living nightmare.

But this was not the end of it. The Germans ignored a promise they had made to the *Judenelteste:* that with the deportation of these ten thousand, the so-called resettlement would stop. Every day they demanded new victims. And our *Elteste* provided new deportation lists for the Germans. The names on the lists belonged to the unemployed and to the employed who at one time or another had received *zasilek*, (financial support).

Even if one member of a family had taken *zasilek*, the whole family was placed on the list. Because of lack of living quarters in the ghetto, three or four families lived together in one apartment. If only one person in the apartment had taken *zasilek*, all of its inhabitants were placed on the list for deportation.

Thus the deportation net entrapped ever larger and larger circles of the ghetto population. And as it did so many went into hiding. Life in the ghetto became a cat and mouse game. People ran from one hiding place to another until they were caught or, exhausted, gave themselves up to the police. So the spring months came and went, with deportation after deportation.

The summer brought some reprieve to the despairing survivors. They mourned their deported parents, children, relatives, and friends; but just as other mourners have to try to forget the dead to be able to go on living, so too the ghetto people did this. They went back to their work, to their everyday problems, their everyday suffering. Then around August, rumors about a new deportation began to surface. No one knew what face or shape this deportation would take. But it did not take long to find out. The "action" started with harrowing bestiality by the Gestapo, who, with the forced help of the Jewish police, rounded up children, elders, the sick, and the weak. The action lasted several weeks, and before the people had a chance to recover from this shock, a new blow hit the Lodz Ghetto.

It was struck early on a sunny morning, September 1, 1942—no human being who lived through the harrowing experience can forget this date. The Germans, with the aid of the Jewish police, drove up to the doors of all the hospitals in the ghetto at exactly the same time and loaded all the patients into trucks. The patients, who till then were better taken care of in the hospitals than other inmates of the ghetto, could not have dreamed of the cruel future awaiting them. They might even have been dreaming sweet dreams when the savage hands grabbed them, and threw them into the trucks like sacks of potatoes, one on top of the other. The SS men blocked the streets so that no one could escape. Within ten minutes they evacuated all the health institutions. Any patient who protested or even asked a question was shot on the spot, as were relatives who broke through police lines, pleading to say a last farewell to their loved ones. In many cases the SS men maliciously allowed parents to join their children and vice versa, and then loaded them together on the trucks. From the way the Germans treated them, there could be no doubt that these people were doomed.

A handful of patients escaped. By endangering their own lives, some doctors and nurses hid a few of them. A woman with an abnormal pregnancy, an open womb, ran and hid. After the action was over her life was saved. Another woman, after a complicated stomach operation, jumped from the second-floor window and hid out until the danger was over. Two thousand patients, including four hundred children, were taken away.

The Germans demanded that all the children in the ghetto be added to the "transport," which was to comprise twenty-four thousand victims. Rumkowski knew that this would be a hard nut to crack. Mothers would not give up their children easily. The Germans depended on Rumkowski. He always tried to please them. But this demand might be just too much.

Anticipating trouble, Rumkowski called a general meeting of all the inmates of the ghetto, and all who were able to came to hear him. I found a place on a crate. I could see his eyes when he spoke. And I could hear every word he spoke. His words are even now like spikes in my bones, and like a fire in my soul. Rumkowski did not ask for "much"—he requested that the mothers and the fathers give their children to the Nazis and that everybody give up their sick in keeping with the spirit of Jewish history, in which at times part of the people had to be sacrificed in order to save the rest! (And the seven heavens did not tremble. The seven heavens hid behind a cloud of wrath.)

Can anyone, sitting in his or her comfortable home, surrounded by children and grandchildren, comprehend the impact Rumkowski's words had on the mothers, fathers, and children who were present during his speech?

Here is some of that speech as it was chronicled word by word:

> "... perhaps this plan is devilish, perhaps not, but I cannot keep from uttering it: Give me those sick and in their place we can rescue the healthy. I know how dearly each family, especially among Jews, cherishes its sick. But with such an edict, we have to weigh and measure; who should, can, and may be saved? Who has the prospects of survival, and who cannot be saved anyway.
>
> We live, after all, in the ghetto. Our life is so austere that we don't even have enough for the healthy, much less for the sick. Each of us keeps the sick man alive at the price of our own health. We give the sick man our bread. We give him our bit of sugar, our piece of meat, and the consequence is that not only does the sick man not become well, but we become sick. Naturally, such sacrifices are noble. But at this time we must choose either to sacrifice the sick man, who not only has no chance of becoming well, but is even likely to make others sick, or to rescue a well man. I could not mull over the problem for long. I was forced to decide in favor of the well man. I have therefore given orders to the doctors that they will be compelled to turn over all the incurably ill in order to rescue in their stead all those who are well and who are able to live.
>
> I understand you, mothers, I see your tears. I can also feel your heart, fathers, who, tomorrow, after your children have been taken from you, will be going to work, when just yesterday you played with your dear little children. I know all this and I sympathize with it. Since four p.m. yesterday when I heard the decree, I have utterly collapsed. I live with our grief and your sorrow torments me, and I don't know how and with what strength I can live through it. Now I must tell you a secret: they demanded twenty-four thousand victims, three thousand persons a day for eight days, but I succeeded in getting them to reduce the number to twenty thousand, but only on the condition that this transport will include all the children up to the age of

ten. Children over this age are safe. Since children and old people add up only to thirteen thousand, we will have to meet the quota by adding the sick as well.

It is hard for me to speak. I have no strength. Help me to carry out this action. I tremble. I am frightened at the thought that others, God forbid, might take this task into their own hands.

You see before you a broken man. Don't envy me. This is the most difficult order that I have ever had to carry out. I extend to you failing and trembling hands and I beg you: give into my hands the victims, thereby protecting a community of a hundred thousand Jews . . . !'"[1]

From thousands of Jewish hearts, a bitter wailing soared up to the vault of heaven. The whole ghetto wept, streams of tears flowed from the eyes of the listeners. But the heavens did not shake; they were mute.

At the end of his rambling speech, Rumkowski announced that an "indiscriminate deportation" would take place. He promised his subordinates, policemen, firemen, and other strong men, whom he appointed as "soul snatchers," that their children would be exempt from the deportation if they did a good job. In consequence, if these people ever had an ounce of mercy in their hearts, they lost it thereafter. They turned into unrelenting fanatics in pursuit of their "duty." They turned into animals.

A street curfew was imposed on the entire ghetto. For seven full days the Gestapo, Kripo, and the Jewish Police went from home to home selecting Jews for death. Those who tried to evade this selection fell under German bullets.

The people in the ghetto were staggered; yet they did not adhere to Rumkowski's words. Mothers did not give up their children, and the healthy did not give up their sick. So the Germans took charge. With their typical brutality, they seized not only chidren and sick people, but victims at random, for having gray hair, for being too short of stature, for having too many wrinkles, for walking erect or for walking bent. The slightest resistance was met with gun fire. You could hear gun fire all around you. Many hundreds of people were shot. It was an unforgettable nightmare. But the worst was yet to come.

[1] Joseph Zalkewicz recorded this speech in his book *Days of a Nightmare* The Lodz Judenrat. Chaim Rumkowski's speech, Friday, September 4, 1942.

The Germans had stepped in to carry out the action because they weren't satisfied with the slowness of the Jewish police. Mothers did not want to give up their children; they put up a tremendous fight, while the children, who understood the situation, went into hiding. And there were cases where the Jewish police were attacked. To insure that the Jewish police would be more effective, the Germans provided them with "iron letters" exempting their children from deportation. This begot a tougher attitude in the policemen when they met with resistance. Now that the reward for carrying out a job was the safety of their own children, they turned into brutal animals. And as had happened before, the Germans succeeded in pitting Jew against Jew, demoralizing and breaking up the Jewish community.

But even the brutal conduct of the Jewish police did not stop the mothers from fighting. Most of the time the police were stronger. And when they themselves could not handle the situation, they called on the Gestapo for help. The Gestapo did not fight or wrestle with the mother who resisted. They just shot her without saying a word. The screams of the mothers and the cries of the children mingled with the shots of the SS men and shook the gates of heaven.

As the horror continued, the ghetto went into a state of paralysis. The fear and anxiety were unimaginable and are indescribable. Still, neither the Germans nor Rumkowski were satisfied with the deportation. The operation was gruesome, but not gruesome enough for the Germans. To placate them, Rumkowski devised a new plan—house arrest for all the inhabitants of the ghetto! The indoor curfew would continue until the quota was met. He named the operation "the Shpero."

The ghetto lay captive. A crushing silence prevailed in all the streets. Only the heavy boots of the SS men and the Jewish police and firemen were heard there. Block after block was encircled with trucks, and the hunters went from apartment to apartment and dragged out the sick and children. Mother and child were shot if either protested; however, if the mother wanted to accompany her child, she was allowed to. Both mother and child, or children, were then thrown together into the same truck.

The trucks were busy until late in the night. They took all the children to one deportation center. The children cried, screamed, called for their mothers. Some tried to escape but, guarded from all sides, none could get away. All of them perished.

When the Nazis saw that the children and sick would not satisfy the quota of twenty thousand Jews, they started to round up Jews of all ages and conditions at random. They chose *mee le'chaim u'mee la'movet*, who should live and who should die, as it is written in the prayer of the High Holy Days. The Germans entered a house with shouts: *"Alle rous!"* (everybody out). Those who weren't quick enough were shot in their beds, or wherever they happened to be. Those who went out were lined up against the wall like cattle ready for the butchers. One German with a sub-machine gun stood on the truck, another searched the house, and a third picked out the people from the line. The Jewish police helped to search the hiding places. These scenes were repeated day after day for seven full days. All during that time no food was distributed. The only thing available to us was water.

The dead bodies were collected and thrown in a heap in the cemetery, where there was no one to bury them. In the meantime, those selected for death were held in the empty hospitals. Because the bodies in the cemetery began to decompose in the heat, the Germans fearing an epidemic, ordered them immediately buried. Grave diggers and laborers were given permission to leave their homes to dig graves.

All through the Shpero, the cooperatives and food distribution centers were closed, and all the vegetable stands were deserted. The hunger was dreadful. The numbers of the sick and dead soared during those seven days. I recall that once or twice potatoes were delivered for distribution to our cooperative, and despite the curfew, lines sprang up. People took the risk, for they were dying of hunger. However, before the distribution started a car with four SS men arrived and shots were fired. Some people in the line were hit, some were dragged to the trucks, and some escaped. This was the way the distribution ended in the Shpero.

Until this very day I am still haunted by the shattering horror of the Shpero. We lived on an edge of the ghetto. Ours was the seventh and last section to undergo the action of the Shpero.

The Germans had divided the ghetto into seven sections. Each day they operated in a different section. The chosen section was sealed off and surrounded by SS men equipped with sub-machine guns, rifles, and rubber truncheons. Trucks were stationed in close proximity. The Jewish police were ready and eager to carry out each order of the SS men. By command, the Jews were assembled in an assigned area in a single line. The "selection" was done in a hurry. With no time to waste, they decided who should die and who should live. The people selected were thrown on the waiting trucks. Those who were spared remained in a state of shock, dazed, disoriented, and crushed. They were tormented by the cruel loss of their dear ones. Almost all families were brutally torn apart. An agonizing darkness spread over the ghetto, the night the seventh and last day of the Shpero was over.

During that night the thought of getting some potatoes became an obsession with me. The hunger was so tormenting, and the fear of long lines was so unbearable that I couldn't fall asleep. I was scheming how to carry out a plan. During the Shpero, rumors had spread that the fields in Marishin were being left unguarded. If I got there early in the morning, before the guards had a chance to occupy their posts again, I might find something to eat.

I was never an "organizer" in the ghetto. I was a *shlimazel*, a klutz. I couldn't even push myself into a queue. I wouldn't fight if someone pushed himself in front of me. And if somebody cursed me out in the line after I told that person he had unjustly got ahead of me, tears would flow, speech would drown in my throat, and I would return home without any ration, while this person got the last available. At home I sobbed, exhausted physically and spiritually. I dreaded the queues. I dreaded my clumsiness and dreaded the thought that I had to go back to the same queue over and over again. For the seven full days of the Shpero I didn't have to stand in line, but being starved for seven days was even worse.

Not only I but my whole family was starving. All of us were swollen from drinking water all the time. During the Shpero I had heard of people running to the fields in Marishin, to get potatoes and beets. Now I would do the same. I would prove to myself that I was really not a *shlimazel*. I would bring my family potatoes or beets so that we would not die of hunger. True, the Shpero was over and the distribution of bread would start again, but so would the queues. No thanks. I thought anything was better than that.

The fields in Marishin were garden plots, bits of vacant land the ghetto people cultivated to produce a few beets or radishes or, with luck, some cucumbers to quiet the painful hunger. Rumkowski distributed these lots, called *dzialki*, among the population. Generally, each person received fifteen square meters, but some were allotted as few as six or seven square meters, and not all of them in Marishin. There were also many who, for no reason at all, didn't get any distribution of a stony lot.

Those who were lucky enough to have a "piece of land," tore the stones out of the ground in Marishin or in the courts where they lived, and after a hard day's work would tend their bit of soil. This arrangement applied to the common people of the ghetto. The "privileged class," on the other hand, was treated differently.

The privileged were those with *protekcja*, (pull) in the ghetto government, or with contact with somebody in a leading position in the ghetto. These special people were called *shyshkis*. From Rumkowski *shyshkis* got large vacant lots, all on Marishin. They also had servants who cultivated these lots for them and guarded their property. They came into possession of their lots long before the general distribution for the plain folks took place. These noble people of the ghetto never knew what hunger meant. They might have known it from before the war, because many *shyshkis* were less than privileged before the war. Some had even been criminals. It was well known that the *shyshkis* lived on the rations of the poor. A great anger rose up in me against them and the injustice of the ghetto. I decided that what I was about to do would be my vengeance against them. So early in the morning I got down from my bed, found a red pillow case to fill with potatatoes or beets, or whatever else I could find in the fields, and woke my sister and told her about my plan. She liked my idea very much. We dressed quietly so as not to wake father, and left the house.

The ghetto was still asleep. The streets were empty. The sun had barely slid out from behind the horizon. The birds amused themselves with merry songs knowing nothing of the calamity which hung over Jewish heads. We walked, each of us occupied by our own thoughts. My feet were swollen and the walk was tiring. From afar we could see the area of the fields; however, the green of the fields was gone. At first we didn't realize what had happened. My sister sized up the situation faster than I. "You see" she said, "there are people who are smarter than we. They got there ahead of us, and now the fields are empty."

But it didn't make sense just to go back after our long journey. "Maybe there is still something left for us, too. Anyway, we are already here, let's try," I said, though I scarcely believed my own words.

We went into a field and started to dig. The effort at first was disappointing. However, after a while I found a small potato, then another one. Happy, I called out to my sister. She showed me that she had dug up three potatoes. I became cheerful. Not all is lost, I thought to myself. At least we will not come home empty handed.

Then suddenly a car appeared. From the back seat window a man shouted in our direction. Neither my sister nor I could make out what he was saying. But since it had been just the morning after the Shpero, I had a sense of danger. I felt the man was warning us. But it was too late.

The car was way off, but I could still see the man's face turned in our direction, while he gestured frantically with his hand. Before this car disappeared from sight, another came speeding in our direction. This time I watched for its approach with alertness. The same thing happened. Again a man in the back seat leaned out, and this time I heard what he was shouting: *"Uciekajcie! Uciekajcie! Schowajcie sie!"* (Run! Run! Run and hide!) Before I had time to look around I heard a lound rumbling of heavy vehicles. From behind this second car a cluster of German trucks came into sight. Only now I realized the gravity of the situation. The Germans, with their bestiality, weren't yet ready to loose their net around us. Officially the *Shpero* was over. I had thought I had survived the selection and would have some peace now. But here were these hunters right in front of my eyes once again. Had I gone through the horror of the action, to be liquidated here in the field together with my sister? Wouldn't it have been better to stay home and starve than to have brought my sister to this field to perish with me? Wouldn't it have been better if this miserable life ended a long time ago? Such thoughts raced through my mind, as about fifteen trucks came to a sudden halt on the road, literally a hundred feet from where I was standing. SS men jumped out of the trucks, instantaneously began firing at some people. Exposed, without any shelter in sight, the people ran into the open field, the Nazis with machine guns at their heels.

This experience is so vivid in my mind that I can still feel the exhaustion in my body, the heaviness of my swollen feet, the dryness in my throat, and the sense of resignation to my fate. I had run about a hundred yards when my body became too heavy for my legs, and I was about to sit down on the grass and let myself be shot. I heard: "Chanka! Where are you? Run! He is right behind you!" It was my sister's voice from very far away.

When she came to a cross-road and didn't see me, she became very frightened. She had been running with the other people while I had lagged behind. I saw her back as she resumed running again but I couldn't match her speed. By now my legs were dragging the two lumps of lead which were once my feet. I forced myself forward for my sister's sake, because I saw her now waiting for me, while the bullets whizzed through the air over our heads. I kept stumbling over every step. She noticed my situation and became terror stricken. In the last second, before I slumped to the ground, our eyes met. I saw her jump and squat, jump and squat, and nervously wave her hands in the air. Then with her fists she beat her chest, her legs, her sides, while she continued jumping and squatting, stooping and bending. The sight has eaten itself into my mind, so that whenever I think of my sister that day I see her crazy dance in front of my eyes.

I motioned with my hand for her to run, and not wait for me. She then started to beat her head with her fists, and jump, jump, jump in one place. I motioned, with my hand, for her to turn to the left. She did not move. She just stood there, while the shooting went on. People were falling to right and left, while she remained standing in place, waiting till I could reach her. The whole episode must have taken only seconds, but to me it seemed an eternity.

When I got close enough to her so that she could hear my voice, I shouted to her to turn left and not follow the others. But she did no budge. Now I could hear her saying again and again: "What shall I do?! What shall I do?!" I answered: "Run left! Only left!" She didn't obey me. On the contrary, she started to jump more vigorously, letting out frightful shrieks. I then realized that she was afraid to move all by herself and leave me behind. With great effort, I picked up my heavy feet, and when my sister saw me moving, she seemed to relax. She turned and started to run to the left while keeping an eye on me. Where the road cut through an elevation on one side, she stopped and waited till I reached her.

To this very day it is beyond my comprehension how it was that my sister and I didn't die in that field of Marishin. Was it that the Nazis became blind and did not see us? Or was it that they did not care about one or two girls when they had a larger number of adults to shoot at? Once I reached my sister, she supported me with her own body and helped me to move ahead.

"Where should we go?" she asked. I drew a deep breath to control myself and said more to myself than to her: "Since everyone is running ahead, it does not pay for the SS men to follow us, who are only two." This seemed to calm her down, and I, by voicing my own thought, became more relaxed too.

In the distance we could still hear the shooting. And when we dared to look we could see the murderers shooting randomly ahead. We moved farther and farther away from them until we reached an area where, to our left, there was high grass and, to our right, a long brick factory building. Now we were actually hidden from the eyes of the hunters. They could see us only if they came up close behind or in front of us. My sister kept asking me if I knew what I was doing. She thought that it was not good to be separated from the others. Should the hunters see us, we had no chance whatsoever of getting away. I thought just the opposite.

My instinct told me—in the ghetto logic never worked—not to follow the fleeing people, that it was better not to be part of a crowd. Then all of a sudden we heard shots in our direction. We started to run once more. I couldn't keep up with my sister, but she did not let me go. She dragged and pulled me—I do not know where she gained the strength to hold me so—refusing to be separated from me again. But when we came upon a narrow path to our left, and I made a movement toward it, she would not follow me. She wanted to run straight on.

"No!" I said, and with all the strength left in me pulled her toward the path.

"Why?" she asked me. "It is no good. We do not know what is there," I answered.

She pointed to the cluster of little houses ahead of us. "These houses are resorts, the work shops. Nobody is working there now. We can use one of them for a hiding place."

"But that is precisely why we shouldn't go there. Others are probably hiding there already. The Nazis will definitely not overlook a place like that."

We spoke in whispers. We were afraid that someone might overhear us. We had hardly proceeded ten steps when we heard the sound of bootsteps. My sister became hysterical. Her body started to shake and she gasped for air. She froze and did not or could not move.

Is she really paralyzed with fear or is it her stubbornness? I wondered. Then she mutely pointed in the direction of the houses. "No! No! No! We are not going there." I said through clenched teeth. "Even if we wanted to we cannot do so now, because just to cross the open field is dangerous. They are not far behind us." I pulled her to one side.

The sound of the booted feet, although not yet close, was nearing. My sister looked backwards. I looked for a miracle.

To orient myself, I also looked around. To our right was an open area of demolished houses, behind which was a wide road, separating the ruins from the resorts. To our left was a stretch of tall green grass. While looking toward the grass, I noticed about five yards in front of us a clearing of about a square yard. I said to myself: This is our miracle. To my sister I whispered, "You are coming with me now."

"Where to?" she asked.

"There," and I pointed to the clearing. She did not see what I saw, but she followed me, anyway.

In a couple of seconds we were in that miraculous clearing, as if it had been reserved for us in that crucial moment. I immediately fell to the ground, while my sister reluctantly did so. The shoulder-high grass gave me a feeling of safety. "Stay down," I said to my sister. "We will lie here until the danger has pased." She wasn't pleased with the idea. The grass was wet. I thanked G-d that she was wearing a green coat, just the shade of the grass. I lay in the dampness and when I heard the bootsteps come closer, I pulled my sister lower by the collar of her coat.

Now, both of us were against the downy earth, but we were protected by the dense high grass separating us from the road. We could hear the SS men close by now. They were running, and at one point we actually saw their outstretched rifles. They must have seen somebody, for one of them shouted: *"Halt! Donner Wetter! Halt!"* and fired shots. Then they passed and silence engulfed the field.

My sister became impatient. Every so often she raised up her body. I had to keep a check on her. She wanted to get up. I, on the other hand, had no intention of moving. Till now we hadn't exchanged even a word. We did not know how far the troopers were from us. After almost an hour of quiet my sister asked, "What will happen now?" Even today I cannot forgive myself the answer I gave her. But I was only sixteen, and she was one and a half years younger than I. Only afterwards did I realize how cruel my answer was. I just said what I was actually thinking at the moment. "Since they suspect that people are hiding here, they will set up machine guns along the road and kill everyone they see." My sister became hysterical and started to whimper. I pulled her over to me and put my palm over her mouth.

"Al tiftakh pe le'satan," Give the Devil no chance to harm you, goes a saying. I had a chance to put it into practice minutes later. I had hardly calmed my sister down when I heard a noise in the grass. I looked to where it came from, and saw the SS soldier just five yards away, his rifle ruffling the tall grass back and forth, as if he was looking for people

who might have hidden there. A cold sweat covered my body. I drew my sister closer to me. I wanted to spare her the grim sight of the armed beast, but it was too late. She had seen him just as I had. She was petrified. I thought, Please forgive me for bringing the Devil!

It took forever for the soldier to walk away. Now the stillness of the field was broken by the sound of a motorcycle, which drove up in front of the resort houses and stopped there. Then a line of trucks rolled up behind it to the same place. We could see people being dragged from the houses and thrown on the trucks. Some were beaten mercilessly. Others who resisted were shot. I saw a young woman with a baby in her arms. It looked as if she was pleading to save her little baby. She and the baby were shot.

When the trucks were full, they were driven off. Ten minutes later they came back empty. The deportation center must have been close by for them to return so soon. In all, forty trucks full of Jews were deported from the resort area. When no more trucks returned, I decided the Nazis had finished their action. And indeed, soon afterward we heard loudspeakers announcing: "*Akcja skonczona!*" (The action is ended!) Upon hearing this my sister jumped up. I had to pull her down again. I did not trust the Nazis. I sensed that it might be a trick. I made my sister promise that she would not move from where we were until . . . I did not know until when. I just knew that we could not go yet.

Again my premonition proved to be right.

The hunger in the ghetto drove the children into the fields. There they dug in the earth for whatever they might find. Sometimes they found a shoe, and sometimes a pot, or a cup, or a rag, but when they dug very deep they found the roots of trees. They gathered these along with fallen twigs and sold them in the streets. Almost on every corner one could see a child sitting on the ground, summer and winter, displaying his wares. And because there was no wood or coal in the ghetto to keep warm or to cook with, people who could afford to used to buy these children's roots. Because there was a market for them, more and more children— and even adults—took to the fields to dig. They dug deeper and deeper, creating vast pits. At the time of the Shpero the pits were almost three stories deep. When the diggers could dig no further, they excavated the sides of the pits, creating caves around them.

When the Germans started shooting at the people in the field, many of them fled and hid in these caves. After the announcement over the loudspeakers that the action was over, these people, including a great number of children, came out of the pits. They were chased in the fields like wild animals. All of them were rounded up and put on trucks that were hidden behind the resorts. These people had held out for seven days of terrible hunger, only to succumb to a trick. It was as the prophet Amos said: "If a man fled from a lion, a bear met him, and when he went into a house and leaned against a wall a serpent bit him" (Amos 5:19).

Thinking about these unfortunate people, I completely forgot about my own situation. I was especially pained when I saw how the Germans handled the children. If they had just not come out of the pits, they would have been saved! Now my anger turned to the Jewish police, for I had a feeling that the Germans would not have known about these hiding places if these traitors had not informed them. From where I lay I could see the whole field. Before the announcement, I could not see a single SS soldier. But when the people and the children came out of the pits, the soldiers seemed to sprout out of the earth. Like hunters, they fell upon their prey. With clubs and bayonets they beat their victims savagely. Like wild beasts, they caught the children in their paws as if they would tear them to pieces.

The shouts and the cries were earsplitting. At a whistle, empty trucks reappeared once again. And once again victims were thrown into them in a hellish fury.

My sister and I lay on the ground and shivered. She embraced me, pressing her body against mine, and uttered a prayer of thanksgiving. "Oh, G-d in heaven, in Your mercy, You answered my prayer and allowed us to escape from the enemies who lay in hiding ready to pounce upon us!" And I answered, "G-d Almighty! Will there be no end to our suffering?"

Only a miracle had saved us this time from the bloody murderers. The sun was high in the sky. It was noon. A relative calm spread over the bloody field. We got on our knees and looked around. We saw that the field guards had taken up their positions at the borders of the field. This was a sign that the Germans and the Jewish police had left the field. We picked up our two bags with the five small potatoes. With heavy hearts we started for home. When a guard stopped us, we just looked at each other, handed over our potatoes, and continued walking.

The Shpero was not to be the last deportation. Every few months there was a new one, and each deportation had a name. One was a deportation of "singles," persons with families or with small families;

another was a "random," for people caught at random and taken away; then there was a *shtichtag* deportation, which gathered up those who had missed a particular day of work. There was no respite from the deportations until the entire ghetto was liquidated.

We had been in the ghetto eighteen months when my mother fell ill again. She started to spit blood, but she hid that fact from us. When she coughed she said that it was a cold she could not get rid of. She did not tell anybody that she was running a fever. Finally, she could not hide her condition any more. She became bedridden. I used to sit on her bed and cherish every sight of her. Every day, every hour, every moment I could look into her eyes, touch her, feel her close, I felt whole and my existence had meaning. I actually felt that her life was a gift to me, a gift I feared might be snatched away soon. I saw death moving closer and closer as she was slipping away day by day. One Saturday morning I raised her up to make her more comfortable. She leaned on my arm, turned her head to one side, let out a faint sigh, and then her head slumped over my arm and that was all. Without any struggle she gave up her soul. She was forty years old.

• • •

"You . . . You have to be my mother now." These words uttered by my younger sister threw me into a sudden shock. I could not react because the words drowned in my tears. I sincerely wanted to help her but I was fighting my own despair. The loss of my mother took away my desire to live. But how was I to react to alleviate her profound suffering, when I found myself in the same dilemma?

Life in the ghetto was bitter and miserable. But as long as my mother was alive, I found purpose in my life because I felt needed by her. She was in need of constant attention. I, in caring for my mother, found life worth living. But now, when she was gone, my courage to go on and struggle evaporated. I found myself in a void. I felt like a snuffed-out shadow.

All the seven days of mourning, I lived as if in a dream. I saw nothing but emptiness all around me. I couldn't think of anything but the past. When flashes of reality hit me, I became paralyzed with fear. I refused to confront the facts of existence. I was weary of the wretched life that surrounded me.

I dreaded facing the morrow. I dreaded the idea of going back to work. The thought that my mother would not be waiting for me at the window, or even in bed, horrified me. On the eighth day after my mother's death, I did not get up in the morning. I wrapped myself in the blanket and remained in bed all day.

Then, when the semidarkness of the twilight engulfed our small room, I dragged myself down from the bed. Once again emptiness surged before my eyes, and my courage to get up collapsed.

My grief, which had been choking me for eight days, welled up and constricted my throat. I covered my mouth with my palm and subdued my tears. Who can help me in my despair and who can alleviate my suffering? The one who understood me most was gone forever.

"Tonight is *stichtag* (fixed date). If you don't go to work you might get on the list." My sister's voice startled me for two reasons: first I wanted to forget about my work altogether, and secondly because I had not heard my sister's voice since my mother died. She plainly refused to talk. I did not answer because I did not want her to see my tears.

I remained in bed. But the warning of the *stichtag* lingered in the air like a whip. After a while I forced myself down from bed and started to dress.

Only now I noticed how shabby and torn my clothes were. It was almost three years since I had a new dress. My mother used to fix my dress and coat. Who will fix them now?

A flicker of a match from across the yard illuminated our little room diagonally. Its narrow ray landed on the door where, on the third and largest nail, my mother's black coat with the silver fox collar hung. After a couple of seconds the light from across the yard went out, but in my mind's eye I could still see my mother's coat with the silver fox collar. It looked new, not faded and not patched. Even the sheen hadn't lost its luster. In the darkness and without realizing what I was doing, I walked over to the door and very gently took down my mother's coat and buried my face in it. A feeling of warmth and security suddenly engulfed my whole being. I felt that this coat was a link to my mother. Her scent penetrated and spread to very corner of my bones. I felt immersed in her presence. My sister switched on the light. She was all dressed up and ready for work. She took me by the hand and like a child I let myself be led by my younger sister.

Outside, the gloomy ghetto opened into a moonless and starless night. We walked hand and hand in silence on the desolate road leading to Marishin. I had a mysterious and distinct feeling that my mother was walking along with us.

Like always the stagnant and suffocating air hit my nostrils as we entered the Straw Resort where we worked since its establishment. The foul odor was a mixture of the rotten straw and the sweat of the gigantic human machine.

We took our stand at our usual places, one opposite the other. Each of us was absorbed in our thoughts. My sister had her eyes fixed on her braid, while my eyes were fixed on her fingers. I always admired her skillful braiding. In her hands the most brittle straw was transformed into silky threads. The inspectors used to call her work "Salusia's Golden Braid."

Although my eyes were resting on her braid, my thoughts were very far away. Suddenly I noticed two large tears dropping on her braid. I looked up into her eyes and I realized that the grief over the loss of my mother extended beyond me.

I wanted to comfort my sister. I wanted to say something but I did not know how. The thought of bringing out what was in my mind paralyzed my tongue. However, I mentally resolved to do something to alleviate her anguish.

The bell rang. We folded our braids and left for home. Outside the purple dawn gave way to a golden morning. Why, I thought, looking at the gigantic sun, can such a fiery ball slide out with such ease from that mysterious yonder, while for me it is so hard to express just a few words that weigh so heavily on my heart? Oh, how I would like to tell my sister how I feel about her! How I understand her.

The longer we walked, the more powerful our silence became. Suddenly my sister nudged me. I stopped and looked into her huge frightening eyes. It was clear that she wanted to say something. In a broken voice, she finally stammered out: "You, you have to be my mother now . . ."

I froze from the sudden shock. I looked at my little sister and I understood. For the first time I realized now that I was so engrossed in my own grief that I forgot my sister's suffering, which could have been alleviated by mutual communication. And only when I embraced her trembling body did I realize that I had been wearing my mother's coat all through the night.

This new awareness filtered out from some unknown mysterious depth, and it pervaded my senses. I looked up at the sky and envisioned a new era, a new beginning. This new consciousness enabled me to take in my younger sister's towering pain.

The fact that I was needed by my younger sister gave me some purpose in struggling for life. Yet, it was not enough to sustain my emotional balance for long. The loss of my mother was too great and my sorrow was too deep to allow me to go on living in our day-to-day ghetto conditions. From time to time I lapsed into apathy and lost the courage to fight. Not having anyone with whom to share my suffering, I turned inward and became melancholy. I lost my will to live.

My father became concerned. He had lost the wife he loved dearly. He did not want to lose his oldest daugher, too. He wanted me to live, to fight for my existence. He did not want me to give up and resign my future.

Once, when only he and I were at home, he walked over to the window I was sitting by and said: "I am going to get married." I was startled. I couldn't believe what I had heard. My father getting married two months after my mother's death? It was insane! Impossible! It was cruel! When he saw me looking at him open-mouthed, he repeated in yet a louder voice, "I am going to get married!"

I went berserk. I jumped and started to tear my hair violently. He slapped me across the face. And before I had time to let out a scream he slapped me again with all his strength. Before I hit the floor, he caught me in his arms, held me up in front of him, and for a long time looked into my eyes. His own eyes were full of tears. He pulled me to his chest and held me tight for a long time, then he wept.

It was the first time I had seen him cry. Both of us brought our grief to the surface. He made me realize that sorrow was not mine alone.

My father's declaration had not been true. It was a calculated provocation to shock me out of my deep depression and bring me back to reality. From then on, whenever we had a chance, we spoke of mother. He told me many stories about her, and I told him how much I missed her. More than once we cried together. We understood each other. He taught me not to forget what I had lost, but at the same time not to forget to appreciate what I still possessed.

The man standing at the far left is my father.

Religious articles of deported Jews were collected and handled in a special department run by Baruch Prashker. Here phylacteries are being checked and put in order. At the far end a Jewish policeman is examining a pair of phylacteries.

5. Resistance

Hitler was not the first one to employ the system of ghettos for the Jews. In medieval times, Jews were often segregated and compelled to live in special streets or quarters of a city. Some ghettos became an expression of Jewish solidarity; there were times when Jews themselves asked to be enclosed in one area to protect them from gentile hostility. There were both walled-in ghettos and open ghettos, and some were better protected than others. When Jews were persecuted, the safest place for them was usually the ghetto. There, they could live their own cultural and productive life without interference.

The ghettos created under the Nazi regime, however, were different

In Marishin:
The straw resort workers eat outside, sitting on the straw.

in character. The sole function of these ghettos was the extermination of the Jews.

Hunger was the great plague of the ghetto. It was a chronic disease which destroyed the victim's body and mutilated his mind. The stomach totally absorbed his consciousness in all waking hours. The pain of hunger oppressed and deprived one of peace, and robbed one of balance in behavior to the extent that the central focus of existence became food.

However, there was among us a small group of religious Jews, most of them young, who disregarded the tragic reality of the world around them, including the hunger they suffered. They hungered more for spiritual food and trained themselves in the art of self-control over the powerful demands of the body. My brother was one of these people.

He was twenty years old when we came to the ghetto. The intolerable conditions, especially the brutal hunger, made people change their way of thinking in terms of religion, but not my brother. He refused to alter his standards and values. He was less concerned with his physical survival than with his spiritual survival; wouldn't change because our conditions changed. He clung to his own convictions.

The shock and trauma of having to leave one's home and possessions and start a new life in the most terrifying conditions was enough to take away the will to live. The hunger, cold, and disease were enough to break any human being physically. But some Jews fought back.

Until the liquidation of the ghetto, the Jews didn't have an organized resistance movement, but it would be a mistake to think that they did not resist the Germans. They resisted on a spiritual level, their chief weapon being their strong will to live. They fought their own depression and their own resignation in the framework of groups they belonged to. To say that there weren't people in the ghetto who were crushed under the weight of the iron hand of the Nazis would be denying the truth. When people lost all, they easily lost themselves. And when they lost themselves they resigned themselves to their fate. They lost the desire to struggle, lost faith in a future, lost touch with the world. Then either they died or went voluntarily to deportation, which amounted to the same thing. But there were others who didn't succumb, and Benjamin was one of these.

Uncompromising by nature, and always ready to fight for his convictions, he joined a group of young Talmudists. They studied the Talmud from morning until late evening. Members of the Hassidic movement before the war, they remained loyal to the Hassidic tradition. Beside sitting and studying Torah in their *shtibl* they organized a special group meal. Each member of the group brought what little food he had received as his ration and put it in a common bowl. Then all ate while singing and telling Hassidic tales. I envied their communal meals. I knew that they could turn a meager supper into a feast with their enthusiastic spirit, songs and tales. It amazed me how this Hassidic group was neither broken nor frightened nor confused but, rather, full of hope.

One event in this connection is still vividly etched in my mind. It was a time when my mother prepared a "festive" meal for the group, a *se'udah shelishith*, the third meal eaten before the termination of the Sabbath. It consisted of a piece of bread and some potatoes my parents and we children had saved every day of that week. I was very excited and impatiently waited for the Sabbath to come.

I also remember when my brother gathered some friends in our house to make a *seuda*. When I first heard that they were going to make a *seuda*, a feast, I couldn't believe my ears. Where would they get the food? I knew from prewar times that a *seuda* is not the work of one person but a collective undertaking. Everyone brings his own contribution to the meal. All the food is put in one dish so that no one will know what the others have brought. Before the war there were affluent Jews who could afford the finest food, and there were other Jews who literally starved all week, and both kinds shared together. But in the ghetto, where nobody had food to spare how could anybody put away even the smallest amount of food for a *seuda?* I thought that it was a crazy idea. But since I had no say in the matter I kept my thoughts to myself. I was sure that they were just talking about something that they could hardly carry out. But I was proven wrong.

The following day I saw my brother cut off a piece of his slice of bread. He wrapped it in a handkerchief and put it in a corner of the drawer. He continued doing this day after day, until he had saved an amount equal to several slices of bread. My mother contributed two potatoes, a kohlrabe, and a bit of flour, and cooked them as a soup. She also saved him some beet leaves. She fried these in a little *zhepak* oil, which in the ghetto tasted like fried fish, and the *seuda* was ready.

Benjamin separated a corner of our room with two blankets forming an L-shape. There he fit a table and four stools. From the attic above us he took down four boards and improvised four benches. Before the other young men came, my sister and I helped him set the table. We still had a white tablecloth. We put the food on the table, the bread, the potatoes, and the "herring" my mother had made out of the beet leaves, a real delicacy.

At the appointed time ten young men arrived. Each brought some food. All the food was placed on a tray, and I thought that they would start to eat. My mouth was watering. I couldn't see how they could wait with the food on the table. They sat down at the table, but to my great amazement instead of eating, they started to study. My brother had prepared about three volumes of the tractate they were learning at that time. With only three books among them, they managed to have a lively discourse. I wondered how they could resist the food on the table, but then I realized that food wasn't the most important thing to them. They became so deeply involved in their Talmudic discussion that they forgot where they were. They had ascended to a different plane!

After they had finished studying, they washed their hands and started to eat. Even when they ate, their minds weren't on food. They sang Sabbath songs to Hassidic melodies. Their enthusiasm kindled a spiritual light in our house. For a moment I was swept up in their ecstasy. For a moment I too forgot my hunger. They were captivated by their own Hassidic melodies, which expressed faith, trust and devotion in the

Almighty. The songs, the meal, the young Hassidim were like something out of a dream. The fervor of faith that came into expression at that gathering made me forget for a while the horrors of our everyday life.

Soon they were swept onto their feet in a dance of unimaginable ecstasy. They rose up to even higher spiritual spheres. They lifted themselves out of the ghetto darkness. I watched them in puzzlement, which slowly changed to envy. I envied their courage and I envied their spiritual strength.

From behind the blankets I could see their faces, their glowing eyes, and their flushed, hollow cheeks. To me they were as saints or heroes, divorced from the present, above it. They were in a spiritual realm, much closer to heaven than to earth. After the young men left, I realized that this gathering had actually been an act of rebellion. The young men had defied their enemy. Despite suffering, fear, pain, and hunger, they did not despair; they did not lose their faith in G-d or in the Torah. They were unique.

Instead of following the orders of their oppressors, they followed the orders of the Torah. They were able to find strength, meaning, and light in the darkness that enveloped their young lives. Their faith enabled them to fight the common enemy—despair and resignation—so widespread among the young ghetto population.

They lived in this fashion until the long arm of the murderers reached them, or the deadly arrow of starvation took their lives. Few of them survived the war, but my own brother did not.

I am still searching for an answer as to why the wound called Benjamin somehow causes such pain to this very day. Why do I hurt more when I think of him than when I think of all the others who were lost in the war? The torments of my soul and the stinging pain in my heart are deeper when I think of him than when I think even of father and mother. Is it because he died so young? Is it because he married in the ghetto? Is it because I later found out that his wife was pregnant? Is it because he suffered so much before he died? He worked as an *efacalia* (human excrement) carrier. I was ashamed of this, but I was only sixteen, four years younger than he, and such things meant a lot to me then. Only one thing is important now; my peace of mind was stolen the day he died.

Perhaps my answer is that Benjamin's suffering reflected the suffering of all Jews in the ghetto, and that for me he represents our entire tragedy.

How was one supposed to perceive the act of marriage in the ghetto? Could this be looked upon as an act of rebellion, too? Was this another way of defeating despair? Was it still another proof of my brother's faith in G-d? In the future? Being a teenager in the midst of death and despair, I was confused when I heard that my brother wanted to get married. A wedding in the ghetto where the Angel of Death is king? I couldn't put my thoughts in any perspective. Some inner voice told me that something was wrong. I had a strange premonition that Benjamin was making a mistake. But, these were only feelings. I did not have one valid argument to oppose the decision of the "grownups." And there was nobody I could tell how I felt. I could not express my doubts to my parents or my brother, and my sister was surely too young to understand.

At the appointed time the wedding took place. It was a religious ceremony followed by a dinner according to the ghetto circumstances.

And then after the wedding everything seemed to go wrong. Benjamin and his wife never came to visit us, and at this time my mother died. Benjamin and his wife came to the burial ceremony. This was the last time I would see Brucha, my sister-in-law. I came back from the cemetery to an emptiness, my mother was gone forever, and my brother . . .?

One afternoon in the early spring, my sister came home infuriated. She was angry at my father. "Why?" I asked her. She didn't want to say. Not yet. After a while she started to cry, and neither my father nor I could stop her crying. Only when she finally calmed down did she start to talk.

She told us that while walking on Dworska Street, she saw Benjamin ("my only brother!") harnessed to an *efacalia* barrel, an excrement container on wheels. The excrement was taken from the latrines in the apartment houses and carried through the streets of the ghetto. Then it was dumped into ditches at the end of Franciszkanska Street. As she spoke, I could feel her pain and her shame. Quite often when I saw an excrement carrier, I could not look him in the eye, for fear that I might see somebody I knew.

"The snow was melting and his feet were dripping mud. His wooden shoes were wrapped with rags for protection on the icy streets. His feet were trampling the melting snow, the barrel was leaking slush, and his face was dripping sweat. Harnessed to the barrel, he was bent double. His face almost reached the ground."

My sister was crying bitterly, accusing my father for letting such a thing happen to "her brother." the shame and humiliation she felt were his fault. I listened and my heart wept. Father drew my sister close to him, kissed her on the forehead, wiped her eyes, and said: "Dear child, I know now what I did not know before. but I know something which is even more important. I know that when you starve, you die. Humiliation and shame are terrible feelings, but you do not die of them. I love Benjamin and I want him to live."

My sister looked into father's eyes and embraced him as he concluded: "Humiliation can be forgotten, but not the death of a young child." She understood and calmed down.

Now there was something else that I understood. After the wedding ceremony, which took place in Brucha's house, I had noticed two *efacalia* barrels standing behind a tree in her back yard. It was clear to me why her family were so eager to marry off their daughter in such difficult times: they needed another laborer to walk their barrels.

Usually whole families worked together at this job. But although they received extra food rations, they usually did not stay alive for long. However, fighting starvation, the longing to survive a little longer caused people to do all sorts of unpleasant things. The additional soup or the extra ration of bread was not enough to provide sufficient nourishment and the back-breaking work, with constant exposure to and handling of human waste, made these workers easy targets for all kinds of disease. Therefore none of them lasted very long. When there were no more volunteers for this kind of work, it was given as a punishment to those who had broken the Ghetto laws.

I went to find my brother, and when I found him, we only exchanged glances. Not a word was spoken between us. There was no need for words; words had lost their meaning and were too narrow to hold my pain. I wrapped him in the blanket which covered his bed. He took up so little space, just skin and bones, a skeleton with flaming eyes. They expressed wonder and gratitude. He couldn't understand how I had found out about him, and where he was. It was father and not I who had thought that Benjamin needed help.

The steps leading from his door to the street were covered with snow, and his walk was uncertain. I held him around the waist; I almost carried him, he was so light! My heart ached when I recalled how robust he had been, how full of energy and strength. Through the blanket I could feel his body shivering. When we reached the sidewalk I breathed a sigh of relief. Thank G-d we made it, I thought to myself. The walk to my house should have taken only twenty mintues, but it seemed to take ages.

My father's face became ashen when he opened the door. On the table a hot glass of tea was waiting for Benjamin. In the corner opposite the door, the bed was made for him. What would mother say if she could see her Benjamin now? This was her only son, her *Kaddish zoger*,[2] how proud she was of him.

"Sit up! Breathe! Stop! Now, turn around! Cough! That's good! Now lie down and rest." Berger, the *feltsher* (paramedic) put his stethoscope into the little doctor's bag, pushed away the chair, got up, left the room, and motioned to my father that he wanted to talk to him.

The door was open. Berger was talking in a whisper. My father had tears in his eyes; also whispered. He seemed very upset. Berger came back, sat at Benjamin's bed again and started to talk to him. He tried to convince my brother that he had no choice but to eat the meat which was distributed once in a while as a ration. My brother thanked him for his good intentions, but explained that it was impossible for him to follow the advice, for according to the Jewish law horse meat is a forbidden food.

"But in your case you are allowed to eat this meat, for health reasons" Berger argued. "Even though this might transgress a commandment."

"Can you assure me that I will not die if I eat the horse meat?" Benjamin asked.

"I cannot assure you that, but you are in very bad shape, and whatever you can do to get better, you should," Berger answered.

"But if I do not get well and I die, I will then die with a defiled body. I will not pollute my body with *treif* (non-kosher food). I would rather die than live, knowing that my soul was poisoned with *treif*."

Berger looked at my brother in amazement and walked out. My father walked over to Benjamin's bed, leaned over him and in a low voice asked, "Benjamin, maybe you would reconsider."

"No," he answered. "I would not eat *treif*, for I feel that I'll choke

---

[2]Kaddish, a prayer said by a son for his dead parent. Kaddish zoger, a son, whose obligation it is to say kaddish for a whole year after a parent's death.

on every bite I put in my mouth." My father didn't insist any more. He looked into the radiant eyes of his dying son and tears fell from his own eyes.

Although the meat was very important for Benjamin's health, Benjamin also knew that if he transgressed one law he would also transgress another. To him it was a question of violating a deeply ingrained principle in exchange for possibly saving his life. The first time it is hard to break a law, but the second time it is easier. In the Ethics of the Fathers we learn that one transgression draws another in its train, and one sin leads to another. This is exactly what Benjamin was afraid of: that he might slide into a habit of sin. The hunger was so great, and also the temptation, that only a superhuman will power could have maintained such control. Benjamin was determined not to budge in his beliefs, nor to alter his way of life.

From day to day his physical condition deteriorated. However, spiritually he climbed higher and higher. He studied the Talmud vigorously. He memorized many pages, and wrote extensively on what he read. He was also in an elated state of mind, which expressed itself in singing *zemiroth*, songs that are usually sung on the Sabbath between the courses of the meals. Although there were not many courses on the Sabbath, yet he continued singing. In other words, he refused to let external conditions penetrate to and influence his spiritual world. However, these conditions had a tremendous impact on his physical health. He fell victim to tuberculosis. He was twenty-one years old when he died.

All Jews in the ghetto were faced with a superhuman struggle to stay alive, but for religious Jews the struggle was particularly hard. In addition to all the privations that had to be endured, the observant Jew faced an additional problem of not being able to keep *kashrut*, the dietary laws, which prohibit eating the flesh of animals which do not chew the cud and do not have split hooves—horses for example. Jewish dietary law also forbids eating many kinds of birds of prey. And fowl that is permissible has to be slaughtered in a special Kosher fashion. However, when starvation in the ghetto reached its highest peak, the rabbis of the ghetto turned to the law of the *Halakha*, concerning *Pikuach Nefesh*, the saving of life, which supersedes almost all commandments of the Torah. According to many *Halakhic* authorities, those persons who might save their lives by eating non-kosher food and do not do so are guilty of capital sin. In our Lodz Ghetto not only did the rabbis permit horse meat, but they even ordered us to eat the meat in order to live. In our house we fought till the end of our strength after my brother was dead—until my father permitted us to bring in horse meat. But only on one condition: when we ate the meat we had to say out loud, "We eat this meat not because it is food and we are hungry, but because it is medicine."

Young fecalistim harnessed to an efecalia barrel (human excrement container) on wheels. The fecalistim—as these people were called—received extra food rations but they did not stay alive long. They were an easy target for all kinds of disease.

6. Sanctification of the Divine Name —Self-Sacrifice

The Jews of the ghetto were in a constant spiritual turmoil. Along with the never-ending struggle for a wretched existence our religious faith was challenged every hour of our lives. In view of the bestiality the Germans inflicted on Jews, how could we keep our spiritual balance? How could we go on living and believe in the divine providence when the whole world around us was crumbling? Taking into consideration the constant crisis of our religious faith, there is little wonder that we were unable to stand up to our inner tribulations. We could not help but ask: "Where is G-d?"

The fact that Jews wrestled with the problem of faith is easily understandable. It is in the tradition of Judaism. Abraham wrestled with G-d over the fate of Sodom and Gomorrah; Abraham, who is a symbol of faith in G-d, challenges the Almighty with the words: "The Judge of all earth shall not do justice?" (Gen. 18:25). For a Jew such wrestling with questions is natural, but accepting one's fate as the will of G-d always resolves crisis. Unshaken faith in the Almighty is the essence of Judaism.

One of the pillars of our faith is *Kiddush haShem*, sanctification of the Divine Name. This principle is one of the holiest in the Jewish tradition. It is also one of the major foundation of Jewish history throughout the centuries. *Kiddush haShem* manifests itself in many fashions, the ultimate of which is a readiness to give up one's life for the sake of proclaiming the holiness of His Name. A classic example is Rabbi Akiba.

Rabbi Akiba was one of the ablest of Israel's spiritual leaders. He did not comply with the rules of the Roman Emperor, Hadrian, and went on teaching Torah regardless of a strict prohibition of such teaching by the Roman regime. He was caught, arrested, and tortured. The Talmud tells us that the flesh of his body was torn from him piece by piece with pincers and that then he was burnt alive. Yet, when the time for morning prayer came, he prayed—regardless of the pain he suffered—the *Shema Yisrael* . . . Hear, oh Israel the Lord is our G-d, the Lord is One.

His disciples could not understand how he could praise G-d when his flesh had been torn from his body. They asked him "Thus far?" (Meaning how far should one go in praising Him?)

He answered: "All my life I have been praying the *Shema* and waiting for the moment to come to be able to carry out my prayer of Sanctifying The Name. For, the Torah tells us: 'Love thy G-d with all thy heart, and with all thy soul.' And what does it mean 'with all thy soul?'

His disciples understood that when the time comes, the Jew must be ready to sacrifice his life with love for G-d, and that only when love for the Almighty reaches its greatest height, will the Jew find meaning in giving up his life for the glory of His Holy Name.

The story of Rabbi Akiba is part of a larger tradition. Rabbi Akiba became an example for later generations of Jewish martyrs in Spain, and in other places where Jews would cry out when they were about to die: *Shema Yisrael!*

When the Crusaders attacked cities in Germany, the rabbis would assemble the people and tell them they were going to have to choose between death and conversion. Then the rabbis would teach their community the blessing of martyrdom: how to praise G-d in the last moments of their lives.

There are descriptions of a new form of *Kiddush haShem* which evolved in the Holocaust. The persecution of the Jews by the Nazis was different from all previous persecutions. Then if the Jews gave up their faith and converted, they were accepted by the persecutors. Physically they were saved. The Nazis, on the other hand, set out to destroy the Jews physically as well as spiritually. They had no wish to convert them. Therefore, the Sanctification of The Name, manifested itself in a different way. One example is the conduct of Rabbi Menachem Zemba, Rabbi Samson Stockhamer, and Rabbi David Shapiro. It arose in answer to a direct Halakhic question: whether one may risk his own life, not to save that of another, but simply to strengthen and encourage his bretheren in a time of crisis. The occasion was a proposal suddenly from the highest ranks of the Roman Catholic hierarchy to save the three rabbis by bringing them to a safe hiding place until the end of the war. The proposal was submitted to the rabbis themselves and they had to make the decision quickly, for the Nazis kept asking the members of the Judenrat whether there were still any rabbis in the ghetto.

After a painful meditation Rabbi Shapiro opened the discussion by saying: "Among you, I am the youngest, and therefore my words are not binding on you. We already know that we cannot help our people, but by staying with them and not abandoning them we encourage them and strengthen their hopes. This is the only encouragement we are able to give our brethren now. I simply do not have the strength to abandon these wretched people." After this announcement by Rabbi Shapiro, all of them felt as if a heavy rock fell from their shoulders and their hearts.[3]

They agreed with Rabbi Shapiro's position. The Rabbis Zemba and Stockhamer ultimately were killed. Only Rabbi Shapiro survived.

It is beyond any doubt that the three rabbis were in a spiritual quandary. They had to determine priorities: should they preserve their lives or answer the call of their moral obligation? After searching their conscience, they chose self-sacrifice over self-preservation.

But not only rabbis acted in this manner: many ordinary Jews refused opportunities to be saved because they wanted to share the fate of other Jews.

Doctor Janosz Korczak was an educator and the head of the orphanage in the Warsaw Ghetto. When his children were about to be taken away to a death camp, he insisted on going along with them. He was not called for deportation but he did not want to leave his children alone in their anguish. The children's world was his world. The children's fate was his fate. He wanted to be with them to the last.[4]

There were also tens of thousands of Jewish mothers who went with their children to the gas chambers rather than be spared by "selection." There were brothers who followed brothers and sisters, sisters who followed sisters and brothers, and children who followed parents. Such Jews, besides following their halakhic obligations, remained mindful of their moral obligation.

The concept of self-sacrifice is an inherent part of Jewish tradition. It was put into practice by our first ancestor, Abraham, who followed the

---

[3] Samuel Charney Niger, *Kiddush HaShem* (New York: Cyco Bicher-Farlag) pp. 161-62
[4] Niger, *Kiddush HaShem* p.125.

command of G-d without question or doubt. And because it hallowed, we should not be surprised to see it carried out in the Holocaust.

An outraged SS man burst into a children's block at Auschwitz with a truncheon in his hand. It was a new weapon the SS men used to flog their victims. After a flogging, the victims usually ended up in the crematorium. The children had heard of this weapon, but had never had it tried on them yet. The SS man came over to one of the bunks and told a boy to climb down. The boy did so. The SS man hit him all over his body, his face and his head. The boy had received twenty-five strokes but he didn't cry. He didn't even sigh. This outraged the brute, so he continued hitting the child in a fury, counting many more strokes. He left his victim to die in a puddle of blood and left the block. But the boy wasn't yet dead. His friends tried to revive him, helped him to his bunk, and watched over him. When they saw that he was able to talk, they asked if he knew the reason for his beating. The boy answered, "Yes, I know why. I brought some *sidurim* (prayer books) for my friends, so that they could pray. Even if I had died, it would have been worth it."[5]

It is possible that if that boy had screamed, he might have gotten away with only twenty-five lashes, but he did not scream. Where did such a child obtain such inner strength? One rabbi reflects on the rationale of the martyr who can endure a great deal of physical pain in the following terms:

> He who is slaughtered in Kiddush haShem does not suffer at all... since in achieving a high degree of ecstasy, stimulated in anticipation of being killed for the Sanctification of His Name, blessed be He, elevates all his senses to the realm of thought until the entire process is one and his sense of the material dissolves of itself. Therefore he feels not pain but rather only the joy of fulfilling the mitzva, the commandment.[6]

Accordingly, the boy in Auschwitz was able to numb his senses to

---

[5] According to Zalman Kleinman, a witness at the Eichmann trial in Jerusalem. *Ani Maamin, I Believe*; (Jerusalem, Mosad Harav Kook, 1978) p.114.

[6] I.J. Rosenbaum, *The Holocaust and the Halakha*, (New York: Ktav Publishing House, 1976) p. 62.

the degree that he felt no pain, or if he did feel pain, found reason to endure in his suffering. So too did thousands of others who suffered and endured. Their secret was that although they lived in the Holocaust kingdom, they didn't abandon the Kingdom of the Halakha, the Jewish Law. This pillar of strength gave meaning to the lives of thousands of Jews and lent reason to their deaths.

The Warsaw rabbis who chose death for the sake of giving encouragement and hope to their brethren were performing an act of self-sacrifice which sanctified G-d's name. Doctor Korczak, who gave up his life for only minutes of comfort for his orphaned children achieved greatness by acting in the same spirit as the rabbis. They all thus sanctified The Name. So, too, the boy in Auschwitz who gave prayer books to his friends so they would be able to pray performed an act of sanctification.

Another way of sanctifying G-d's Name in the Nazi era was observing the dietary laws in the ghetto. At a time of sickness, such an act was a manifestation of a strong determination to carry out the practice of the Jewish religion. This in turn elevated the pious Jew to the highest level.

Although the Jew could not carry out the commandment of *Kiddush haShem* in the Holocaust period as in the Middle Ages, the sacrifice was essentially the same. For, the Sanctification of G-d's name is not achieved in death only. Living one's life with meaning and purpose, as a Jew, on the most intense level, at a time when continuously confronted by death, is considered to be no different from public martyrdom.

• • •

"Home! Tower of strength. / Cradle of warmth. / Only those who lose you, / truly know your worth."[7]

In these lines the great Polish poet, Adam Mickiewicz, relates to us the inner meaning of home. We who lost our homes fully grasp the import of his words.

Like all the other people in the world, we too had once had a home. Had once been a happy, loving family. Now not only was our home a

---

[7]Translated from Adam Mickievicz

fading memory, but two of the five members of my family—my mother and my brother—were no more.

The three of us who remained—my father, my sister and I—tried to carry on and share the pain of living a day-to-day life like hunted birds. Death lurked behind every step we took, and suffering filled every waking hour of the day, while the sleepless nights were filled with the torture of constant hunger. Now, it was father who spread his protective wings over us. He remained our lighthouse in the sea of darkness. He was our rock of strength when life around us crumbled into dust.

Now, the threads of my memory weave themselves back to that time, when the situation in the ghetto worsened. Besides hunger, cold and epidemics, one deportation followed another in rapid succession. One selection followed another. My physical and spiritual strength slowly melted away, and my desire to live steadily ebbed. I envied those who didn't have to wrestle any more to stay alive. Now, when I look back at those fateful years, I can hardly comprehend how I lived through that decisive period. One particular blind feeling settled in the center of my being: I would have given up the struggle to stay alive, if it were not for my father. I remember telling myself that I had to live for his sake. Giving up would have been betraying him, and I did not want to forsake him. Conversely, only the warmth of his devotion and protection kept me going. I felt that as long as he was near me no evil would touch me. And in fact, in all the years that he was with us, neither my sister nor I were ever deported or put on a list of deportation. This in itself was very unsual.

The minute a family in the ghetto was broken up, its members fell victim to deportation to an unknown destination. The fact that I had not been deported I attributed to the invisible protective power my father possessed to keep my sister and myself out of danger. He also watched to see that our morale did not dim. He tried to make us understand that to learn to endure pain is to strengthen one's character. He taught us to accept our fate as part of the Almighty's greater design. His moral support made it easier for us to try to endure life in the midst of the Nazi's naked brutality. He preserved for us the last vestige of home.

Shortly before the complete liquidation of the ghetto the list became frighteningly extensive. Everyone who was working in the resorts—shops producing goods for the Germans—was on it, and we were as well. I do not know by what miracle my father got us off the list. Very few were exempted. We were among those few. However, we were caught by an SS man who set two vicious dogs on us, as he clubbed us out of our home with his rifle.

Now after much suffering and struggle even this home was gone. And shortly thereafter, my father too was torn away from us.

By 1944, we no longer believed Rumkowski's promises that deportation meant a resettlement for work. Although people in the Lodz Ghetto lived in terrible conditions, they were reluctant to leave for what they knew was worse. The loaf of bread promised at deportation did not tempt them any more. There was too much evidence that deportation meant death. Everyone in the ghetto knew that Czarnieckiego, the gathering place for deportees, was a place of no return. Orders were disobeyed, and many people went into hiding when it became clear that the liquidation of the people in the ghetto was an established policy and that there was no exit from that tunnel of night. All signs pointed to the last phase of our destiny, the liquidation of all who still remained.

This phase began with the termination of the resorts, those slave factories which made goods for the Germans. The directors of the resorts sought to continue the illusion of productivity, so they invented other work for their workers. Our own director, Farber, for example, sent us to the cemetery. There we were ordered to cut the high grass and make bundles of it. The purpose of the job was irrelevant. The important thing was that we were employed. Although we worked hard—we weren't used to laboring with a scythe—we enjoyed the outdoors. The fresh air and the open sky gave us a feeling of freedom despite the many freshly covered graves. Everyone among us had a part of their family in them. When I looked at this landscape of destroyed lives I was sometimes envious. Am I any better off than they are? I asked myself. And aren't they better off than I am? They are free of the agony of hunger. They are free of fear of deportations. They are at peace.

But in spite of myself, a new desire to live arose in my soul. The horror of our great tragedy had not yet succeeded in destroying my yearning to live. Amid all the gravesites of the dead, my desire to live surged up with an unexplainable force. I vividly recall the thought when I looked at the many thousands of tiny tin markers: Who will tell how they lived and how they died if all of us are dead? I must live at least for that.

One day, deep in thought, I heard a gentle fluttering of wings over my head. It was a bird. I had not seen a bird so near me for many years. It circled around over my head with a loud and sharp chirping. My sister too was looking at the bird. When she caught my eye, she motioned me to come over to her working area, thirty feet away from my own. When I got there I could hardly believe my own eyes. There was a bird's nest and in it five little eggs. My sister, working with her scythe, had invaded the domicile of the bird and caused it to abandon her yet unborn chicks. It made my sister and myself feel very sad when we looked at the still scolding bird over our heads. I had the thought then that the poor creature was just as homeless as we were. We hid behind the high bundles of hay, hoping the bird would return to the nest, but it didn't come back and flew away. We brought the eggs home.

When my sister broke the eggs, she found a tiny chick inside each of them. With a bit of oil she prepared a dish for us. She and I ate it, oil, chick, and feathers together, but my father refused the dish. "I cannot eat it, for I can see and feel the pain of the mother bird," he said. And when we began to eat he wept and said: "This is a real *tzar baal chaim*. May G-d forgive you this transgression."

Now the dying around me took on epidemic proportions and the deportations became a daily occurrence. Every day I heard that one of my uncles, aunts, or cousins had either died or been deported. Often when I went to visit a friend I found her lying on the floor covered with a white sheet, or I found her room empty because she had been deported the day before.

The Talmud tells us about a ship that was caught in a raging storm in the middle of the ocean. The ship started to sink. The passengers were ordered to throw all the heavy, non-essential cargo into the ocean. Among the passengers was a Jew, who upon hearing the order took his bag with prayer shawl and his *phylacteries*, which weighed less than two pounds, and threw it into the ocean. For this Jew the heaviest burden had been his Jewishness. So at first opportunity he threw it away.

I am sorry to have to confess that in the ghetto I was like that Jew. I did not abandon my religion altogether. I adhered to many of its laws, but only superficially; my heart wasn't in it. My faith had been shattered. My once deep-rooted belief had been destroyed, and my orthodoxy as of nought. I think this was so because I was in rebellion against a world gone mad, against a society that had lost every shred of humanity. I was like flotsam on the ocean, drifting without a course.

Although other Jews were in the same situation, not all reacted in the same way. A few of my friends, for example, accepted their fate, without rebellion, as the will of G-d. They suffered the same physical anguish as I did, but their faith in the Almighty was never shaken. They sailed the stormy ocean sure of their direction; they did not occupy their minds with questions that have no answers. They concerned themselves more with keeping their spiritual balance than with the horrors all around themselves. They found meaning in *Halakha*, the Jewish Law, and the purpose of life.

I had two friends who never worked on Sabbath all through the years in the ghetto. To this day I cannot understand how they escaped deportation. One day, returning from work, I met one of them, a girl named Pola. She told me that she was on the list and that she had to appear the following day at Czarnieckego, the deportation center. A couple of weeks later, to my great surprise, I met her again. Seeing my puzzlement, she explained that a miracle had happened to her. In the darkness of night she had managed to run away. But from then on she had had to live in hiding, for the police were looking for her. She said that to find a hiding place was a lesser problem than to get some food, because her ration cards had been taken away.

I was astonished by her calm. By that time she was all alone. Her father, her sister and one brother were dead. Her mother and her other brother had been deported. As a single person she had been a prime candidate for deportation, but somehow she was still here.

The next time I met her, she was in a concentration camp that I had been sent to. There again Pola demonstrated her unshaken faith in the Almighty. Somehow she had managed to smuggle in a *siddur*, a prayer book, and very often I saw her standing and praying. The act of praying in the camp required a tremendous amount of spiritual courage. But what astonished me most was that all during Passover she did not eat bread. Jews are, of course, forbidden to eat bread on Passover, and in normal times they are able to substitute other foods for bread. But in the camp there was no other food substitute and Pola had to go hungry.

Four ounces of bread and a watery soup were all we had for our daily nourishment. I do not know how, but she survived the eight days of Passover. Nothing else but her strong spiritual conviction could have sustained her then, and all through the fury and tribulation of the Holocaust. I remember how small and worthless I felt when I did not find her standing in the line for bread throughout Passover, and how heroic she appeared in my eyes when I saw her again. I can never forget how consumed with shame I was one time when I looked at the portion of bread in my hand and then saw her praying.

I knew that one day the Germans would be defeated, but for us the defeat might come too late. And as for the Messiah, I didn't doubt that he would come, but would he come in our time? I knew that Jews had suffered before. If the Messiah came only because we suffered, then he should have come a long time ago. Since he hadn't then, why should he come now?

• • •

One day, before our deportation, my father took me aside and said; "It seems that the liquidation of the ghetto is imminent. It is also possible that we might not be able to stay togehter. Therefore you must know that should we survive and look for each other, the best thing would be for us to have a sign between us. The sign will be our last name. We will change it to Landlerner, a combination of our and mother's maiden names. And please remember my date and place of birth. It is very important." I didn't ask any questions. I just tried to remember each and every word father had said. Then I started to pack what was still in our possession.

My father was a very particular man: he liked everything to be in order, especially when moving from one place to another. But this time he acted strangely. First of all he didn't help me pack. Then, when I put something in the valise, he would say, "You won't need this," turned around and walked out of the room.

As the liquidation of the ghetto neared its end, we got into a cat and mouse game: when an action approached our neighborhood, we would flee to a neighborhood where the action had already taken place. This went on for about two weeks. Then we heard that the action had moved to a distant part of the ghetto. We breathed with some relief when we could sleep in our own beds. The night passed peacefully, and so did the early morning hours.

Our total food supply at that point, consisted of three beets. Since it was relatively quiet, I decided to cook the beets so that we could eat them in a soup. As I was grating the beets into hot water, my sister said; "It seems that there will be no action today. There are no sounds of the trucks and no shouts of SS men. I'll just go out and check so that we can sit down and eat in peace." And she walked out.

Through the window I saw her crossing the street, then look around. It's a long time since this area enjoyed such peace and calm, I thought to myself. My sister took a few steps forward, toward the chestnut tree, the only one on our block. Then from nowhere a young man appeared. He had a nice smile on his face, and he leisurely approached her. Suddenly two dogs the size of my sister leaped up as if from the earth and fell on her. She started to run, but the dogs held on to her skirt following her right into our home. There they attacked us, jumped from one to the other and tearing our clothes. Then an SS man burst in and began hitting us over the head, with shouts: "*Raus. Raus. Alle raus.*" (Out. Out. Everybody out.) He pushed my father out with his rifle, while the dogs pulled my sister after him. I grabbed the valise I had filled as well as the knapsack I had prepared for my sister and followed them outside. The idea of escaping didn't enter my mind. For how could I leave my father and sister in the hands of the murderers and save my life?

In the early autumn morning, trucks and open wagons loaded with Jewish men, women, and children were moving past us in an unending procession. Each vehicle was guarded by SS men armed with machine guns aimed at the prisoners. No cries or lamentations came from the people in the trucks. Resignation prevailed. My father, my sister and I, were not put on the trucks. We were escorted on foot by the SS man and dogs to the deportation center.

Czarnieckiego was full of people. All were waiting, but nobody knew for what. Each of us was given a loaf of bread, and we joined others who were sitting on the asphalt floor. I was afraid that the bread might be poisoned. Before the night fell we were put aboard a train. We were sealed in a cattle car without any windows or other openings for air to come in. I knew that our fate was also sealed. I couldn't touch my bread.

It became chokingly hot, and there was hardly any air to breathe. I hoped that when the train started moving some air would filter in. However, by the time the train started to move, the stench from the vomit, sweat, and excrement of the many passengers was suffocating. Children cried. Mothers begged asking for help for their children. But no one was in a position to help.

Memory fades; some terrible events discreetly hide themselves in the remotest folds of the mind, only to be brought back to consciousness by a song, a word, a tune, a smell. Many things remain forever hidden but the picture of my father in the train going to Auschwitz has never left my mind's eye.

We were standing in the car, body pressed against body. There was no place to sit. Here and there people lay piled one on top the other. Mothers held their children in their arms. Fathers squatted under the weight of young sons on their backs. Brothers and friends held each other by the shoulders, exchanging positions from time to time. Lack of air, lack of water, and lack of sanitary conditions. For more than twenty-four hours we rode in these conditions making the situation intolerable. The moaning, screaming, and crying of the sick and the children tore one's heart. The pain and suffering all around was shattering. One woman must have lost her mind, for she started to hit the people around her with her fist. A young girl was leaning against the wall of the train and pulling out her hair slowly, strand by strand. Then suddenly she started to tear her clothes off, while banging with her feet against the wall of the car.

All at once, in the midst of this confusion, chaos, and disarray, I heard my father's lovely voice: "*Ani maamin, ani maamin, ani maamin, beemuna sheleima . . .*" (I believe, I believe with perfect faith in the coming of the Messiah.) Then he followed this prayer, which he sang, with encouraging words of hope. He tried to inspire the people so that they would not give into despair and hopelessness. He told them that our sages taught us not to lose faith in the Almighty even when the sword rests upon our throats. But he did not stop at that. He went into an exalted dance. He danced while standing in one place and kept on singing. And then a miracle happened. The children stopped crying, and the women stopped lamenting. Some of the men picked up the tune and joined my father in singing. Everyone's mood changed, although it was clear to everyone that this was our last ride.

I watched some men slowly put on prayer shawls and join my father in prayer. I looked at them and wondered: How is it possible that with so many changes in the world, and with so much time gone by, the situation for the Jews is always the same. Jews were persecuted all through the ages because they were Jews, and Jews are being persecuted now. The men wrapped in their prayer shawls made me think of the history of the Ten Martyrs, and of Rabbi Akiba. And now, almost two thousand years later, right here in this cattle car, Jews are going in their death, praying to the Lord of Israel.

The Talmud tells the story of Chana and her seven sons. Before the

Romans killed her she had to watch all her seven sons being slaughtered. I do not know why thinking of her then somewhat relieved my fear of death. Possibly because she was a heroic woman, and possibly because I had her name. I felt composed.

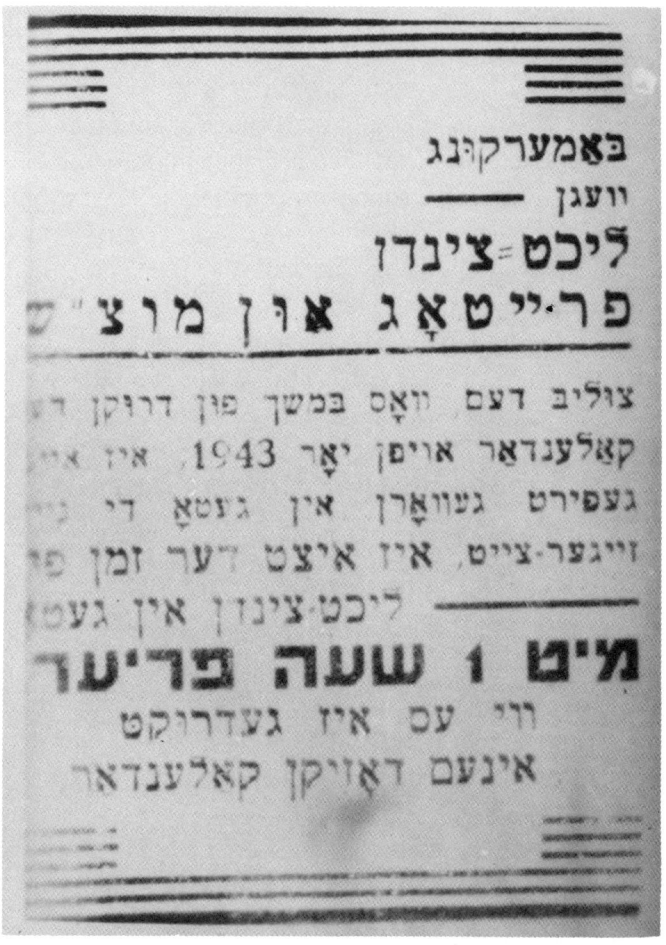

The years of turmoil and tribulations under the Nazi yoke did not dampen the Jewish religion and customs. "Announcement about candle lighting of Friday and the termination of the Sabbath. Because of moving the clock during the printing of this calendar for the year 1943, the time for candle lighting is one hour earlier than printed in this calendar."

7. Auschwitz

Finally our journey was over. The train came to a sudden, jolting halt. Shortly the doors of the sealed cattle car burst open with a frightening bang. The gruesomeness of Auschwitz lay before us.

We were shoved down like bags of garbage. Those who could not jump out of the car fast enought were rolled or pulled out. Those who were completely immobile were thrown aside, and after only a few minutes the place was strewn with human bodies. Those who had not succumbed were lined up in a column of five abreast and, at a rifle signal, marched along a sandy and graveled road. The length of the marching column was endless. We noticed a strange smell, a sharp smell that assaulted our nostrils. Then someone said: "This smell is of burned human bodies." People around me started to weep. And as I looked ahead I noticed smoke rising to heaven from the creamatorium chimney. I noticed flames, leaping flames, and I asked myself if these flames would bear witness to our tragedy.

Then we were halted and ordered to form two columns. The decision as to who went in which column was made by a sign from the index finger of one man. When his finger pointed to the right, the person was pushed with a rifle to the right, and when his finger pointed to the left, the person was thrust to the left. The process of selection was done in the most gruesome and heartless way. Children were torn from their mothers, and if a mother protested or tried to get her baby back, an SS man shot them both. Those who tried to cross from one column to the other were also shot, or set upon by vicious dogs, or brutally beaten, for interrupting a job that was supposed to go fast. The left column was led away immediately. People in the right column had time enough to look around and see the dead bodies of old people and tiny babies. Some of the babies were covered with the bodies of their dead mothers. I can still see a small leg in a white sock and a black patent-leather shoe sticking out from underneath a woman's corpse. Not far away a young boy lay on a bearded man, probably his father, still moving in the last agonies of death.

Auschwitz, that factory of death, lay before us. The angel of death held us in its embrace, and yet I harbored thoughts still of escape. I was shocked out of my fantasy by a vicious dog jumping on me. I then realized that the people in front of me had moved ahead already. I instinctively hurried after them. It wasn't really the conscious me that moved, but only my body. As I was to learn, in Auschwitz even the body was not yours. It belonged to the henchmen of this hell. Pushed and prodded along, I stumbled on the others. Suddenly, a girl from among us started to scream at the top of her voice: "Smoke! Smell!" And then: "Here is the smoke! And the smoke brings the smell!" Her cry triggered a chain of screams and wailings. One could hear distinctly the words: "Here! Here are the shades and here is the soap!" In my naive innocence I did not know what all this meant. But it was the beginning, and I was still ignorant of the reality around me. I soon learned that here the human body was exploited totally: the strength was used for work; the skin was used for lamp-shades, pocketbooks and shoes; the fat was used for soap; and even the ashes were used to fertilize German soil.

We were ordered to form two lines, the men in one, the women in the other. My father hesitated. He wanted to say something to me, but an SS man thrust his rifle butt in his back with such force that he almost fell to the ground as he ran, propelled. When he gained his balance and straightened himself up he looked for my sister and me. I grabbed my sister and pulled her to myself. My father saw us. Our eyes met. "Let's not lose each other," I whispered to my sister as the men behind him pushed my father ahead. After a minute or so I lost him from my sight.

In our desperation my sister and I clung to each other. I held her hand so tight that my own hand hurt. After losing father, all my mind concentrated on just one thing, not to lose my sister. My shoe came off my foot when I stumbled on a stone. I turned to pick it up but my sister pulled me ahead. Then shots rang out. I saw a man tumbling to the ground. I recognized him. He had been in our cattle car. All through the journey he had sat in a corner of the car and prayed. Somehow I had the feeling that the SS man had aimed at me but hit him instead. For along time afterward I couldn't get rid of the thought that I had been singled out to die, but he had taken my death. From that moment on I never looked back. This was not a place where one could look back. One followed the crowd and the orders if one wished to survive.

We reached an intersection on the sandy road and were ordered to turn left. I noticed money on the sand, German marks, Polish zloties, even American dollars. There were gold watches and silver candlesticks. And just a couple of steps farther on bodies were strewn about the place. One man was gasping his last breath, then dropped his head into the sand. Then I saw a young boy almost a child crying over his father's body. He didn't want to leave his dead father. Then another boy—he must have been a capo—grabbed him by the collar and pulled him away. Dead and dying all around me. It looked like a slaughterhouse.

For a moment I thought that maybe I was dreaming a horrible dream from which I would wake up. A blow on my head and shoulder told me it was not a dream. There was a distance between me and the people ahead of me. I pressed my sister's hand to make sure that she was with me. I noticed that my sister's face was white as a sheet. I pulled her and we started to run to join the others. This was Auschwitz, and this was our reality. A planet of smoke and fire, of ashes and gas, a universe of madness where death reigned as king.

The woman in front of me was crying and tearing her hair as she marched. Then I saw everybody around me crying. The whole column was weeping. I could not weep, I could not think, all I wanted was to die.

I saw a young woman was hugging the high-voltage wire fence and I thought, How lucky she is. She is beyond suffering; at long last she has tasted peace. For an instant I thought to imitate her and leave this world behind me. But the thought of death brought with it the thought of my father, whom I could not desert now.

All the years in the darkness of the Lodz Ghetto, I had felt that death would not touch me because he protected me. Through the deportations and selections his spirit had shielded me. As long as he was around, I had been able to endure. Now he was gone, torn from me when we stepped on the bare Auschwitz ground. We had tried to hold fast to each other, but to no avail. I had followed him with my eyes until he disappeared in the ocean of human bodies. Far away I saw a mass of men, but I did not see him. Yet he must be somewhere, and as I had needed him he might have need of me.

Amidst the barks and gunshots, amidst the cries and smoke, my body moved along, a part of the long marching human snake. At last we entered a barracks, where I found myself in the thick of human bodies, naked bodies, all around.

Why are they naked? I asked myself. But before I could think of an answer, a man appeared and tried to rip off my clothes. I put up a struggle and was immediately hit on the head once, then again. I took another look around me and then I understood. As I lowered my skirt, the man tore open my mouth.

He snarled: "Where is the ring? The golden ring? Where did you hide the diamond?"

"I never had a ring." I told him.

"Your mother's diamond ring, the wedding ring?" His questions were like clenched fists banging at me.

"My mother is dead," I told him. "She died two years ago. I sold her diamond ring long before she died. I had to buy her milk and apples, and pay the doctor, and buy vitamins. She was sick a long time before she died. Look, these are her clothes I am wearing!" Now I wasn't talking, I was crying, begging. I was pleading for him to let me go. I felt that I was going out of my mind. His face, his smell, his grip, made me feel that I was losing my senses. Suddenly he ripped open my mouth again, "No golden teeth, ha?" He spat on me, and shoved me ahead on top of another girl in tears. Now I was crying like everybody else. And I was naked like everybody else.

All through the ordeal the thought of my father did not leave me. I longed for him. I felt lost without him. Does he know what is being done to me here in this horrible place? Ah, but what is happening to him? He is in the same horrible place. Are they treating him, my father, the same way they are treating me here? The thought of my father being ill-treated troubled me more than my own situation. As I looked about me, seeing other people abused, and only slowly started to truly comprehend my predicament, the more apprehensive I became about my father. He, too, might now be standing in a barracks like the one I was in.

It was a narrow but very long place. The width of it was five people standing very close to each other. The length of it was indefinite. I could see neither the beginning nor the end of it. To my right there were four girls or women. I could not distinguish their ages nor their faces; all looked alike. Their heads were shaved. Only when I looked at them and touched my head, did I realize that I had no hair. My head was clean shaven. When did they shave my head? Who shaved it? And where was I when they shaved it?

Just beyond the four girls close to my right, was a high blank wall, with no space between it and the last girl. However, between me and the wall to my left there was an aisle the width of one person. There, the men who shaved the girls moved freely with truncheons in their hands. For the smallest offense, like crying too loud, or stepping out of line, or protesting, one was beaten mercilessly. The people in charge were capos, inmates chosen by the SS to do this job.

As I was looking around, I noticed alongside the left wall some tiny windows. When the capo wasn't watching, I turned my eyes to these openings to see what was happening outside the barracks.

Across the sandy yard there was another barracks with similar little windows. Something in me made me stare out at them. Suddenly I saw a man poke his head out of one of the windows. He started to look about to search with his eyes. When he turned straight ahead I immediately recognized the face. "Abba! Abba, I am here!" I called at the top of my voice. "Abba! Abba! Can you see me?"

I do not know if my father saw me, too. I just know that the instantaneous joy was cruelly quenched by a flood of blows to my naked body from a rubber truncheon. Mercilessly, the capo tore me away from the place where I got the last glimpse of my dear father.

A world of monkeys, I thought with disbelief. For a moment I couldn't make out the connection between me and the little monkey boy standing next to me, searchingly looking into my eyes. Only when this little creature burst into tears did I recognize my sister. Had I seen her in the street, the way she looked now, I would have surely walked away from her without recognition.

Thus was my first day and my initiation to the death camp called Auschwitz.

I soon learned that life and death here were dependent on selections. These were carried out every day, and sometimes even twice a day. My sister and I agreed that she would—as long as we were here—always be in front of me at all selections. For, I feared that she might not be allowed to live because she was so small and frail. I did not want to survive without her.

Selection followed selection and each one was a confrontation with death. Who should live and who should die was in the hands of one man,

Doctor Mengele. He looked over your naked body and pointed his stick either to the left or to the right. Those on one side went straight to the gas chambers, while those on the other would live to go through another selection. After the first selection, my sister and I were assigned to block number twenty-five.

Block twenty-five was one of the worst blocks in the Birkenau camp. There was no straw and there were no bunks. There was only a floor of asphalt, wet with muddy water. We were twenty-five hundred girls crowded into a place without room to sit or to lie down. We stood about for a long time. Some of the girls became restless and started to push and shove. Then came an order from the capo to go to sleep. We looked at each other in disbelief. The capos beat us with rubber truncheons, then showed us how we were to sleep. One girl had to sit on the floor, spread her legs and take another girl between them. And so on until we were lying on top of each other, five in a row. The first and the last in a row were the worst off. The first didn't have anyone to lean on; she was constantly sitting while holding a person in her lap. The last, on the other hand, did not have anybody in her lap, but she was usually the first to get beaten, stepped on, and walked over. When a capo wanted to hit any one of us, she just stepped on the last girl and struck at her victim. I was happy not to be one of the first or of the last.

I overheard a discussion between two capos about a transport of one hundred girls from my block to another block. As I listened to them talk, my eyes sought out my sister, and when I caught her attention, I signaled her to come over, and fast. By the time she reached the place where I was standing, the capos had already announced that a hundred people were needed. They didn't say for what, but a voice inside me told me to run from this place, this horrible block number twenty-five. I felt as if someone were urging me to leave, and I started to think of father again.

By the evening my sister and I were in a group being led to block number thirty-one. When I walked into that block I could not believe my eyes. There I saw girls lying on *pritches*, one next to the other; not one on top of the other. There were ten girls to a *pritch*, separated into two fives, and there were five tiers of *pritches*, one on top of the other. No matter how bad, it was still an improvement over the conditions in block twenty-five. I had no doubt in my mind that my sudden decision to go had been guided by the invisible hand of my father. How great was my shock when, the next morning, I found out that during the night block twenty-five had been liquidated. None of the girls I had left survived.

The only improvement in block thirty-one was that here we slept squeezed next to each other instead of on top of each other. Otherwise Auschwitz remained Auschwitz. The selections went on day after day. Then one day Dr. Mengele decided that my sister was ready for the gas chamber. When she approached him, he immediately pointed to the left. I saw that this was the side of death. When I approached him I didn't even look where he was pointing at, I just followed my sister.

This time we were two among five thousand girls squeezed into one block. We didn't receive any food and we just stood up because there was not enough space to sit on the ground. We stood like that for many hours, awaiting the hour of our death.

Before nightfall we were led out. A column of five thousand. The darkness of night slowly descended on the universe of Auschwitz, as our column approached the gas chamber. At that moment I thought of the *Marranos* in Spain. These were the Jews who, to save their lives, had outwardly embraced Christianity while in secrecy they continued to practice Judaism. When they were found out they were brought to the stake, and burned alive while jeering onlookers watched them die in agony. I also thought of the martyrs who, wrapped in the parchment of the Sefer Torah, jumped into the fire crying "*Shema Yisrael...*" "G-d is our G-d, G-d is One!"

That moment is so clear in my mind that I would be able to recognize those faces if I saw them now. They were bewildered faces, but there was no panic. No cries. No fights. Was it resignation, or was it a mute covenant among the people not to yield their dignity in front of the enemy? Or had they become part of the silence and secrecy of night?

While deep in thought, I turned my eyes to the right. What I saw was beyond human imagination: A mural of ivory white bodies the length of that wall of night. In the beginning it looked like a large, still painting. But then I saw eyes, living eyes, flashing out of the painting. I thought that I was dreaming. But I couldn't stop looking. Then I heard the sound of an engine idling. Only then did I realize that these naked bodies were standing on trucks, waiting to be driven to the gas chamber. At once all the truck engines started up and the trucks with their doomed cargo headed away.

After a while I saw heavy smoke braided with glistening sparks rising to the sky. It disappeared before it reached heaven.

Where is my father? Where is he now? Is it possible that he was one of those thousands who just went up to heaven in that smoke, and those sparks? I asked myself. I couldn't think any more. I became impatient and wanted to get into the gas chamber and get my life over with. Only one desire held me now, to join my father and never be separated from him again.

The column was moving closer to the steel gates of the chamber. Now I could see how it was done. The steel doors opened, a group of people were forced into the chamber by SS men. The doors closed. SS men with dogs and machine guns guarding the column. At each cut-off point SS men from both sides drew a truncheon across the line of the first five girls who were waiting their turn.

Suddenly I felt the truncheon on my chest. I knew that my turn was coming soon. I touched my sister's hand, to make sure that she was with me. I tried not to think. And yet I felt that I should say something. Make a wish, beg forgiveness. But from whom? And why? What wrong had I done? I could find no answer to any of my questions. Then my mind froze.

"*Umdrehen! Mach los! Schnell du Schwein!*" (Turn around! Go! Run fast, you swine!) Startled out of my numbness, I could not understand what the SS men wanted. Then I was hit over the head with a truncheon. My sister pulled me and I started to run back with all the others in the column. While running, my sister whispered, "If you act like that again, they will shoot you on the spot." Indeed, I had been lost in my thoughts. It was she who had brought me back to my senses.

We were herded into a building, where we were told to get a bath and be disinfected. Shaken to the core, I couldn't believe the rumors that we were saved from the gas chamber and the crematorium. Others must have felt the same disbelief I did, for suddenly a shriek pierced the stuffy air of the bathhouse, and that sudden outcry was instantaneously picked up by many others, creating an outburst of fearful madness, a roar of despair as from animals being led to slaughter. I caught myself screaming along with the rest, not realizing what I was doing releasing my fears in a collective panic, in an ocean of screams.

The girls who worked in the bathhouse tried to calm us down, saying that for the moment we, indeed, had escaped death. With tears in her eyes one said that she would gladly exchange places with us, that her doom was sealed while ours was still in question. The people who worked in the bathhouses were being replaced every couple of months.

Those who left were sent to the gas chamber because the Nazis wanted no witness to remain alive.

She told us why we had been spared. Just minutes before, an order had come from Germany requesting five hundred slaves. "Better slaves than ashes," she said. "You can still nurture a spark of hope."

After the bath and disinfection, we were each given a dress and a pair of wooden shoes. Some girls got leather shoes. My sister was one of them.

Outside, the trucks were already waiting for us. In the darkness of the night we were being moved to a new destination.

My father came to my mind again, and in my mind I questioned him. "Was this an accident or was it a miracle that my sister and I were saved for the moment? Was it truly better to be a slave than to be ashes?" Then I thought again of the saying from the Talmud: "Even when the sword rests on one's throat one should not despair."

Timidly the morning dispersed the heavy darkness. A new day began to dawn. After riding for about three hours we reached a town. Through a crack in the side of the truck, a world long forgotten appeared in view. A real and beautiful world and yet one forbidden to us. A world of tall trees and manicured lawns, flying birds and circling butterflies. Then I noticed houses among the trees. And a child. A child in a pink dress must have noticed the butterflies. Laughing, she ran out of the house with a jar in her hand, and started to chase after one. Innocent children playing in nature. What sin did our children commit that they were cut off from nature, from laughter, and from life?

When the blackness of night again blotted out this new world, we got down from the trucks and started to march. After about two hours we reached a forest, where five vans were waiting for us. We were herded into them and driven off. But where to? My mind was reeling. We had been saved from Auschwitz and we were going to a concentration camp to become slaves there, I thought. Wouldn't it be better if we had died in Auschwitz? Would there be no end to our suffering, Almighty G-d!

I couldn't think any more. A feeling of resignation and apathy enveloped my soul. I was moving in a cloud. I was indifferent to my surroundings. I just felt a need for my sister. I wanted her near me. I wanted to be assured that we were still together. I saw her pushing herself through a throng of people towards me. At that moment everything went blank. I fainted.

I do not know how long I was unconscious, but at one point I felt the warmth of my sister's body. She was supporting me so that I would not fall. Then with the help of another girl she started to pull me down from the van. I begged them to leave me alone. I wanted to fall into a sleep and never get up again. I didn't want to struggle any more. But they just made me get out of the van along with all the others.

Now, like a robot, I proceeded to follow those in front of me. The warmth of my sister's body soothed me. But I could not grasp what she was saying. Her voice sounded like a muted echo, sounding from a thousand miles away.

We marched for hours. It was a march without an end. Then in the full darkness before dawn we entered the Schrohl spinning factory.

The place was empty and gray. The gigantic room was one big shadow. I was aware of people, but I couldn't make out their faces. When the sound of our movements died down, a frightful stillness engulfed the place. And then a hissing somewhere broke the stillness. Then I realized that the sound came from the ceiling. When I looked up I saw many pipes. I suddenly felt a choking sensation. The pipes seemed to be moving, descending. In horror I shut my eyes, but the sight had already penetrated my mind. A strange odor filled my nostrils. I felt life running out of me.

I do not know the length of my unconscious state. I just remember hearing my sister's voice begging for some water, and then water being splashed into my face. I remember hearing her pleading softly: "Please, Chanka, not here! Not now! Please, do not leave me alone!" And then louder: "Please, let her live. She's all I have left. Please, you can see that she is a strong girl. She can work. She's just exhausted from the long march!"

I recognized my sister's voice, but my mouth was dry and my voice choked off. I couldn't force out the faintest sound. I could feel somebody rubbing my feet, my hands, and somebody holding a wet cloth to my forehead. Then I was lifted up and propped against a wall. I opened my eyes and saw my sister standing over me. Her eyes were filled with tears. (I found out later that she had appealed to the *Kichen Shefin*, director of the kitchen, who had persuaded the SS women not to send me back to Auschwitz, and thus saved my life.) I do not know why I broke down at Schrohl after barely escaping the gas chamber and flames of Auschwitz. But reason made no difference. As the girls later joked, I was the only one who was initiated into Schrohl with water.

Mr. Schrohl, the owner of the textile factory, which was in Halbstadt, needed fifty textile specialists. The price he paid for these specialists was to house and feed five hundred worker-prisoners from an ammunition factory near by. He had ordered the prisoners from Auschwitz. (Shortly after the fifty "specialists" were chosen for the textile factory, fifty Hungarian girls arrived to fill the quota for the ammunition factory.) It is quite possible that the Germans chose five hundred out of the transport from Lodz, because Lodz was a major industrial city and we would be familiar with factory work.

Our camp in Halbstadt was a slave-labor camp. However, unlike many other such camps, it was spared from the deadly "marches" in the heart of winter. In this camp I had a top *pritch*. From there I could see the marchers through a window. Columns of people without end passed by day and night. Wrapped in blankets, they walked without food or drink. I saw them bend down and pick up snow to eat. I also saw them stumble one upon another, and then heard shots and saw them fall down dead. Some lost their shoes and when they tried to pick them up they were either shot or clubbed to death. Such marches were the final phase of life for thousands of victims.

The Germans wanted to hide the cruelty of the concentration camps from the liberating forces. As the front neared, they evacuated the victims, so that there would be no evidence of Nazi barbarity. We were lucky to be spared such marches.

We were at Halbstadt to work, to produce for the Germans. We suffered hunger, cold, disease, lice. We were beaten by SS women. But there was no crematorium there, and there was no gas chamber.

Halbstadt was a universe in itself, a concentration camp with its own SS leaders and its own laws. All of the SS women were extremely cruel except for one named Ushi. Was it because Ushi was intelligent or was it that she had a heart? I will never know. We came to the camp at the end of October, 1944. Germany was losing the war. Ushi's humane behavior toward us was perhaps her protection for the future. In secret, she provided one of our girls with news. That didn't improve the miserable condition we were in, but it helped our morale. When I found out about Ushi I was so impressed, because I saw that in the everlasting darkness there still could flicker the spark of a human soul. On the eve of liberation, the French workers in the ammunition factory warned our girls to behave in the usual manner, for our camp was mined. And Ushi was the one who told us how to behave so that our SS guards did not suspect that we knew their end was near. Any disturbance on our part or any show of happiness would cause the SS women to blow up the camp, we were told. As we found out later, a group of French men were on guard hiding in the cellar of the factory the night of May 8 and May 9, when we were liberated.

In an abyss of debasement, one spark of courage shines like a beacon. That spark for us came from an unexpected source and made my sister and me feel like human beings again.

Our experiences in the Nazi era had made us distrustful. After years of degradation and suffering, it was hard to believe that decent human beings still existed. Living on the level of animals, without minimal human rights and without any protection of law, we could hardly believe that there was anyone in this dark universe who might care for us as human beings.

It happened in Halbstadt, in the Schrohl factory, on the first day of my slave labor. I had been put in charge of a gigantic spinning machine. I had no idea how to work it. Before I had a chance to collect my thoughts and orient myself, a middle aged German woman accompanied by an SS guard came over to the machine to instruct me how to use it. The SS guard watched both of us. I concentrated all my attention on the woman's instructions, to make sure that I could perform each and every step, exactly as I was shown to. I knew that my life depended on how productive I would be. With shaking hands, I took the hot spool, attached the thread to it, looped it through a few holes and connected it to the dangling soft cotton cord. The machine was spinning with a steady rhythm while my head reeled.

In the afternoon, when my machine was running smoothly, I was frightened out of my wits when in front of me, out of nowhere, appeared a six-foot, broad-shouldered peasant woman. If there had been a place to run to, I would have done so. But we were well guarded and there was nowhere to run. So I just stood there, petrified.

When I started to move, she blocked my way and motioned with her eyes in the direction of my guard, putting her index finger on her throat saying: *"Ich und du kaput!"* (I and you are finished!) It was beyond my comprehension why she had picked me out of all the other girls in the plant. My mouth became dry. She kept on talking, but I did not understand any more of what she was saying. She kept on repeating: *"Die

Ohlle, Die Luder!" Although I did not know the meaning of these words, I thought their sound had a derogatory connotation. When she pronounced them she made an angry face at the guards. Now, what was I to do? I was confused and afraid. If she was indeed a friend, and I was caught in "conversation" with her, I could be sent back to Auschwitz. Luckily, the SS woman was sitting on the window sill biting into her fat sandwich. The big peasant woman now lowered her voice to a whisper, squinted with her left eye—I noticed that the eyelids of her right eye were stitched together—threw a look at the SS woman, pointed to her small white apron and with rapid steps walked away. (Everyone had to wear an apron to collect the waste cotton from the machine.) Thoroughly confused, I followed the half-blind peasant woman with my eyes.

Before she reached the door, she turned to the right where the garbage crates were standing. While bending over to throw her waste cotton into the crate, she glanced at the guard and then at me and walked out.

I didn't know what to make out of this episode. Although suspicious, a small voice told me that the peasant woman was not an enemy. Her personality elicited trust, regardless of her ugly and angry face. I calmed down and went about my work, happy that my machine was running smoothly. But after a couple of minutes I noticed that in the front of the machine a spool started to snarl up. As I ran to attend to it, I lifted my eyes, and there in the twelve-by-twelve inch window in the large entrance door, I saw her face again. When she caught my glance her one eye narrowed in a smile. I cleaned up the snarl, but some power drew my gaze to the little window. And there she was, still staring at me with her one smiling eye.

Not knowing what to do, I followed my instinct and imitated the walk she had taken, simultaneously looking in her direction. The minute she saw what I was doing, her whole face lit up and she slowly moved away from the window.

In that gigantic hall, there were fifty huge spinning machines, set up in two rows. On each machine there were two aisles. The work was divided so that each girl had to attend a machine and a half. My machine was the first in the hall. I attended both sides of the first machine and a half of the second machine. From my machine to the entrance door was an empty space of more than a hundred feet. When the peasant woman saw me walking out from behind my machine and heading toward the door, she moved away, but now I saw her again in the little window. A feeling of uncertainty crept into my mind. What if I was walking into a trap? But now, being visible to the SS guards, I could not turn back. One was not allowed just to walk; so I had no other choice but to proceed as with a purpose.

Her face kept disappearing and reappearing in the window as if to convince herself that I was not going to return to my working place. When I turned right, as she had, I saw her face light up with satisfaction.

I proceeded to the crate she had stopped at. The crate was almost three quarters full of white cotton waste. But in the left hand corner of the front I noticed a *V* shaped piece of paper about an inch long. Strange. The crate was to be filled with the cotton refuse only, and only by the Jewish slave-girls. Who could have thrown away a white piece of paper? A piece of paper was a treasure! Even such a small piece.

Slowly I removed the cotton wads above it. What revealed itself was a white package. It felt soft to my touch. My eyes turned to the window sill where the SS *Aufseherin*, had been sitting. I did not see her there. I really got scared. Where could she be? Maybe right behind me? But I was already in the thick of it. If I was caught in a trap, then it was too late to turn back. And the temptation was too great. Maybe the package contained a piece of bread? It felt like a fresh bread. I could not resist that.

With a swift movement I grabbed up the package and put it in my apron. But as soon as this treasure was secure my feet began to tremble. Was it worth the risk? If the *Aufseherin* caught me, my punishment would far exceed the pleasure. Worse yet, all the others could be punished for my foolishness. My head was reeling.

Then I tore myself away from the spot and returned to my machine. When I calmed down, I relized that it had not been a trap. The *Aufseherin* was not nearby, and nobody knew what was going on in my mind or what was in my apron.

Now my treasure became a dilemma. I could not leave it here for several reasons: the smell could attract others, the *Aufseherin* might inspect my apron—as she often did—and find the package, the package could be traced to the peasant woman, who could end up sharing our lot as a slave. I had to empty my apron at all cost—and fast. I decided to ask permission to go to the toilet. But what about my sister? How could I not share my treasure with her?

Because I wasn't attentive enough, the spools of the machine kept clogging one by one. My sister, attending the other half of my second machine, noticed the problem developing on my side and came running to help me clear up the mess. We were not allowed to talk to each other during working hours. So when she came close to where I was standing and repairing the machine, I took her hand, put it into my apron, and said, "Toilet." She understood what I meant and moved away, but kept on watching my every movement.

Shortly thereafter I asked permission from the *Aufseherin* to go to the toilet. I waited there for my sister. Thirty-three Jewish girls worked on that floor. Only three were allowed to go to the toilet at one time. The minutes until my sister came in dragged on without end. Finally she entered. But we couldn't do anything because there was another girl present. I made myself sick. My sister did likewise and faked vomiting spasms. The other girl looked at us with pity and walked out.

With shaking hands, I ripped open the white package. What we saw there was beyond our imagination: two fresh slices of bread, one white, and one black. Real bread! And in between the slices a thick slab of white cheese! We almost fainted with surprise. But there was no time to admire our gift. Somebody was bound to step in at any minute. I broke the sandwich in half, threw the white paper deep into the opening over which I had positioned myself, and gulped down my half of the sandwich. My sister devoured hers. In no time we were out and back at our posts as if nothing had happened.

Just as my temptation was irresistible before I ate so my puzzlement was incomprehensible now. The peasant woman was not out to trap me. For the *Aufseherin* was not looking for me. Then what was her motive? Was it a momentary impulse of humanity? Why would a woman, a German, endanger her own life for the sake of a Jewish slave-girl? Was it possible that a spark of decency still glowed in the darkness of of a concentration camp?

Just as a pious Jew would not forget to put on his *Phylacteries* each morning (except for the Sabbath) so did the peasant woman not forget to bring me a sandwich with white cheese every day. On Saturdays she brought me a sandwich filled with a kind of blueberry preserve. For seven full months—until the liberation—she supplemented our miserable daily ration in the concentration camp. For months I yearned to exchange a word with her, to express my gratitude and let her know that her kindness kept my sister and me alive.

My sixth sense told me when she was at the door. She, on the other hand, did not come in until she caught my eye and was sure I was free to go over to the refuse crate. It often happened that I was ordered to help out at different machines in different places in the hall, but I always seemed to know when her eye would appear in the little window of the door. Even when I was busy at the far end of the hall, I could see her from between the rows of spools. The instant she saw me, her whole face lit up in a smile. What caused that dear woman to act as she did? I wondered.

Our liberation was as swift as it was unexpected. The Nazis disappeared as if the earth had swallowed them up. We were free! No more *Aufseherins* and no more slave work! No more appels and no more fear, and no more spinning factory! However, I was saddened by the possibility that I might not see any more of the peasant woman. I felt so grateful toward her that I longed to see her one more time so that I could finally express my feelings to her. At night, and often during the day, I used to make up sentences I would speak to her, to tell her that she had not only saved my life, but that of my sister as well. When I formulated these sentences I did not believe that I would ever be able to deliver them. But now free, I was ready to give anything to see her at least once more.

With the coming of the Russians, the Schrohl factory was closed. For hours I stood outside of the building with the hope that maybe the peasant woman would come there to pick up something she might have left there. Or maybe she would come for a payment that was owed her. But she did not return. I decided to go to the village nearby and look for her. I went from house to house, but many people had fled and many of the houses were empty. I stopped people on the road, describing her and her occupation. One evening, when I was particularly discouraged and ready to go back to the camp, I met a girl of about twelve. Hesitantly, I walked over to her and asked the whereabouts of the peasant woman. She knew her well. She lived about twelve kilometers from our camp, the girl told me.

That night I was so excited that I couldn't fall asleep. When the first rays of sun appeared, I woke my sister up, and both of us went out looking for our friend.

The sun was high in the sky when we reached her house. It was more a hut than a house, with a thatched roof and only one window and one door. There was no path leading to the door and no steps before the entrance. It just stood there as if isolated in a wilderness. We knocked at the door. A hoarse voice answered: "*Hereinkommen!*"

I pushed the door open and there she was, lighting her stove. When she turned around and saw me, she left the stove and ran to embrace me. It was a long time since I had felt such warmth. She was so surprised to see me that she almost lost her power of speech. She couldn't understand how I had found her. After a short explanation, I introduced my sister. When she looked at her, she began to cry: "Such a child! Such a child!" she said and repeated, "Such a child!" She made us sit down and have some food with her. We were each given two slices of bread, one white and one dark, and in between a white piece of cheese. This was her invariable lunch. And this she shared with us for seven full months. The house was sparsely furnished with one iron bed, a table with two chairs, a stove and some pots and pans. There was no floor, just earth, and no covering on the dirt floor. In a corner, a slab of wood was connected to the wall. It had six large nails in it, and was used as a doorless closet. In the opposite corner, there were two pails. One was half full with clean water. The other must have served as a waste vessel.

She moved the table to her bed. She told us to take the two chairs. We looked in each other's eyes while eating in silence. She added water to the milk she had prepared for herself and shared it with us. When we finished eating I started to thank her, but she did not let me talk. She said there was nothing to be said. When I blurted out that she had done so much for both of us, she stopped me and answered that she did what she had had to do and flew into a rage as I had seen her do the first time, saying: "*Die Ohlle, Die Ludde!*" in reference to the SS women who guarded us. And as if suddenly in a hurry, she looked us both over, got up and walked out with us.

She brought us to a luxurious house, where she introduced us to the people there. I did not understand what she was saying, but when she finished talking a place was made for us at the table. An elaborate meal was in progress and we were served soup and meat, and fruit cake. We hadn't seen such food for almost six years. Then the hostess walked over to her closet and took out two dresses, one for me and one for my sister.

After we thanked and said good-by to the hostess we told the peasant woman that we would find our way to the camp, but she was determined to accompany us. She talked all the time. I did not understand what she was saying. I could not concentrate on words. I was thinking about this one-eyed woman, how different our lot would have been if there had been more people like her. How many thousands of

Jews could have been saved if the gentiles had not so eagerly cooperated with the Nazis. Hitler poisoned the minds of his people and the anti-Semites of the East European countries had poured out their hate to aid him in his demonic ambition. Few and far between were those who were able to preserve their humanity amid the universal madness, and one of these was the peasant woman.

In 1944, as the battlefront moved closer to the gates of Lodz, the final liquidation of the ghetto began. More than 60,000 people were sent to Auschwitz-Birkenau between June 23 and the beginning of September of that year. Only 800 people were left to clean up the ghetto. After they did this job, they were ordered to the cemetery to dig their own graves. They dug eight graves about seven feet wide, seven feet long, and about five feet deep, in which they were to be buried.

After the war, when I came back to Lodz, the first place I visited was the cemetery and the graves of all my loved ones. There I saw the eight open graves. They were empty.

By the time the eight hundred who were left to clean up the ghetto had finished their digging, the darkness of night had fallen. The murderous guards, wanting to play with their victims a little longer, let them suffer another night of anguish, had secured them in the memorial hall behind bolted doors.

None of the prisoners expected to live beyond the next morning. But when they saw that the sun was up and they were still alive, hope raced through their hearts. The following night—January 19, 1945—they were liberated by the Russians.

The Lodz Ghetto did not experience any armed uprising as did the Warsaw Ghetto. There was not insurrecton of desperate people who had nothing to lose as was the case in other Jewish communities in Poland. The reason for this was that the Lodz Ghetto was totally isolated from the outside world. The Germans sealed it off more hermetically than any other ghetto in Poland. All attempts at contact with it by the Jewish underground failed, and the Polish underground in the area was too weak to do anything. The Germans, on the other hand, were most successful in camouflaging their plans in sowing confusion among the victims. Rumkowski and his staff were an efficent instrument in the German hands for blunting opposition among the ghetto inmates, and implanting in them the illusion that obedience to orders and observance of a strict work discipline would save them. The tragic fact was that Rumkowski could not save the ghetto, nor even himself, when his service to the Germans was ended. Like all the other victims, the Germans used him up. When they sent him away to Auschwitz, they gave him a sealed letter to the chief of the camp and assured him that he would, or course, be treated in a special manner.

When he and his family arrived in Auschwitz, they were the first from their transport to be thrust into the gas chamber.

When my aunt left the room my uncle handed me this picture saying, "Anna, please hide this picture so that your aunt should never see it again..."
I recognized my two little cousins, Alusia and Ryvcia who were so brutally snatched away in Shpero.

8. Liberation—9 May 1945

One night when I returned from my regular shift I felt an unusual change in the air of the camp. I could touch the tension in the darkness. Something unexpected was about to happen. But what?

For weeks there were rumors circling about an evacuation of our concentration camp, as had taken place in other concentration camps. For weeks, through the windows, we saw people wrapped in blankets marching barefoot in the snow, stumbling, falling and being shot. Now, I thought, our time of marching has come. A girl pulled me over and whispered into my ear: "Behave as if nothing has happened. Keep silent. Go to your bunk. Cover your head with your blanket. Make believe that you are asleep. Tell the others to do the same. Our camp is mined, and sub-machine guns surround the camp. Any sign of emotion or commotion can cause disaster."

We knew that the marches were a sign of the German capitulation. We also knew that the Germans wanted to leave no evidence of their acts of atrocity. They could blow up or burn down camps and evacuate the victims so that no sign of them remained. I was wondering if I would live to see our liberation and the Nazis defeated.

These thoughts were on every mind that night. No one slept. But each made believe that she was sleeping.

Peeking out from beneath my blanket, I could see a very unusual commotion. The head of our SS guard was running back and forth with her dog, giving orders to the other SS women in a hushed voice. They packed and carried boxes and packages as if they were moving out. Even in defeat, the Nazis stood by their idea of order. The following morning, as if nothing had happened during the night, we were ordered to stand in *appel* (line) and be counted. But we weren't ordered to go to work! We were just left standing. A shiver went down my spine when I heard the girls whispering the name "Houptman." Houptman was the SS leader over all the concentration camps in our region.

Just a few days earlier, Houptman had come to our camp with his two big, black dogs to punish one of our girls. The SS guards had found her with a piece of paper and a pencil. Instead of shooting her, Houptman gave her twenty-five lashes on her naked body. Now, we thought, he is coming to carry out his final punishment.

He came without his big dogs and walked into our barracks. He looked around, got up on one of the bunks so that he could be seen by all, and with his head bent and looking at no one, but just staring into space, announced: "You, my dear children," he stopped to gasp for air, "you are going home now. The war is over. You are free. You have a future. But what will happen to me I do not know." He got down, straightened up, and one by one ripped the medals off his chest. He started to cry and then walked away.

I noticed that Houptman wasn't armed. I also noticed that all the SS guards were gone by the time he had finished his short speech. Was it right that we should let him go? Why didn't we take revenge for our suffering? I, who had suffered six years at the hand of the Nazis, felt pity for this defeated man! I cannot understand why. And although I felt angry at myself for feeling as I did, I was sure in my mind that I couldn't have harmed this man. I could not have made him suffer. He was a human being. We were five hundred and fifty girls. Not one of us ran after him. Not one of us tried to hurt him. Why?

Was it cowardice on our part? Or was it heroism? The man was unarmed. All the other Nazis were gone. We weren't frightened of them any more. What did Houptman think of our Jewish girls?

That night I had a terrible dream, a nightmare. I saw my father and my mother disappearing and reappearing again. But I never, all through that dream had the feeling that my father was dead.

In my dream, Nazis with dogs chased after my father. He had no place to hide. They caught him and led him to a waiting train. When the train started to move, I ran after it. The train picked up speed. I was desperate to run faster, but the more I forced myself the less my legs obeyed me. Then, as if nailed to the ground, I started to shout, to call out to my father. But I was choked up and no sound escaped from my mouth. I forced myself to pull myself from the ground, but the ground became quicksand, and I began sinking. I saw the train become a gigantic snake as it descended from the mountain. A strong wind came and brought with it a cloud of locusts. When the cloud came closer and stood over my head, it lifted me up, and I became part of the cloud. Now, the cloud, with me in its midst, chased the snake, and when I looked down I could see puffs of smoke boil and hiss from the snake. I looked closer and saw father. He was wrapped in his prayer shawl with the shining ornamental collar, sitting among monsters and criminals, who were his students. His face was shining as with the golden rays of the sun. In his hands he held a heavy volume of the Talmud, from which he was instructing his students. Each word he uttered became sparks which flew up to heaven and circled G-d's seat. My father's face slowly dissolved; only his eyes remained. I started to tremble because I did not want him to disappear. I started to cry and call: "Father! Father!" But mother appeared and then my father's face returned. I knew that my mother was dead, and when she tried to touch me I moved away from her. But I stretched out my arms when I heard her saying: "Don't be frightened, your father is a *Zaddik*, he will protect you and . . ."

I must have screamed, because I felt my sister shaking me and asking: "Who must be alive? Who will protect you? Chanka! Chanka! Wake up! Wake up!"

The following day my sister and I started to search for father.

The first thing we did was to look for him in other camps in the surrounding areas. Mainly, we visited liberated camps for men. We were full of hope that we would find him. Eight kilometers from Halbstadt there was a men's concentration camp, a small one with eight hundred men. We spent a whole day there inquiring if some of the men knew or had seen father. But to no avail. Nobody knew a man of his description or name. However, there we found out that about thirty kilometers away there was another very big but terrible camp. Early next morning my sister and I started out for it.

In those early post-war days there was no public transportation. However, my sister and I decided that we had to go and visit this camp, where thousands of men had lived, languished, and died. Maybe G-d had provided a miracle allowing my father to escape the murdering hand of the Nazis.

We walked. We walked from village to village, asking people whom we met on our way if they knew the location of a large concentration camp. My feet were so swollen, that after walking for a few hours we had to stop. My feet became heavier and heavier. We had to rest often. Night fell. We slept on grass not far from the road. We jumped to our feet, and ran to the road next morning when we heard a wagon. The wagon stopped and picked us up. I prayed to G-d that He would help us find father. From afar we noticed a man in a striped coat, a *muselman*, a walking skeleton. I told the driver to let us off.

From that *muselman* we found out that indeed not far from this point there was a *lager* called Schathousen, a horrible death camp where many thousands had been killed. Yet there were still some *muselmen* alive. He was one of these walking corpses. He also told us that at this camp there was a list, a register, of all the six million Jews who were killed by the Nazis. This was the first time that I heard this specific number. My sister started to cry. She didn't believe that we would find our father alive. I, on the other hand, still hoped. I had reason to believe that my sister was wrong: father was young and healthy and he had a tremendous will to live.

A truck driver going in the same direction allowed us to ride with him. One hour later we were at the gates of Schathousen.

In Auschwitz, thousands of people were gassed and burned dead and alive every day for many years. There were special factories for this purpose. There were open pits where children were burned alive. People were clubbed to death, shot, tortured, hanged. They were used for medical experiments. Even if one would live for a thousand years one could never erase Auschwitz from memory. Auschwitz was a devouring beast. Once there, no human being could dream of getting out of that all consuming hell. At Schathousen, we saw what was beyond human imagination; we saw piles of dead bodies two stories high. People on the top of the pile were still moving, some on the fringes of the pile were moving their hands and feet. A world of corpses. And the people who were walking around looked as if they had just risen from that pile. They were walking corpses. I did not believe my eyes. It was a world of death and moving ghosts. I saw four or five such skeletons walking, then fall to the ground and die. Just like that. They did not even realize they were liberated. They were too weak to care.

At a distance of about fifty feet from the mountain of human bodies there was a wooden shack. Just one foot below the sloping roof there was a series of very tiny glass windows. Here and there boards were missing from the wall. The entrance was wide open, and people were sitting on the ground with gigantic books, leafing through the pages. Most of the people were crying. These were people like us who had come with hope in their hearts to find a loved one and almost all were disappointed. My sister looked at me without words. A wave of sorrow filled up my throat.

All the hope I had nurtured till that minute evaporated. I walked over to the table at which a kind of secretary was sitting and signed my name. I too was given a heavy book. It contained names. Hundreds and hundreds of pages of just names. These were names of people who had perished, and also of people who at some point had passed through this camp. I didn't want to start with the letter L, with which my father's name began, for fear of being quickly disappointed. I also thought that by starting from A I might find the name of somebody from our family who had passed through Schathousen.

Finally, after going through three books, I reached the letter L. I was now leafing the pages very, very slowly, because the names were dancing in front of my eyes. Then, suddenly on the top of one page, the actual name of my father leaped up. I pointed it out to my sister and we looked at each other in disbelief. Was he one of those who had perished? Thanks be to G-d, no! Next to the name the date and place of his birth fixed his identity unmistakably.

My sister pointed to another date. February 17, 1945, he had passed through this camp. I embraced my sister full of excitement. My sister, on the other hand, was full of tears. I asked her: "Why are you crying now? If father passed through here two and a half months ago, there should be no doubt in our minds that he survived. Right? By now he might be on his way home to Lodz or already waiting for us there."

My sister looked at me in puzzlement. She turned her eyes to the mountain of dead bodies, then gazed at a couple of walking *muselmen* who had collapsed in front of us. I knew what she was thinking, but I did not cry.

How our friends envied us. We, at least, had a hope to hang on to. My sister and I packed our possessions and started out on the road.

Not having any means of transportation, we proceeded on foot. And whatever kind of vehicle we met up with, we asked the driver permission to ride with him. Some kilometers we traveled by truck, some by horse drawn wagon, and some even by a jeep. When we were on Polish soil, we were told that there was a possibility of boarding a train. For more than half a day we walked until we reached the station. But there were so many people at the station that it was almost impossible to believe that there would be place for all of us on the train. For a moment I thought that our effort to reach the station was in vain because some people had been waiting here two days. At nightfall the people started to move closer to the tracks, as more and more people streamed in from all over the surrounding area. Everybody tried to get as close to the tracks as possible. We were no exception. Late afternoon the next day the train finally arrived. Now the real action started.

Pushing and shoving, pulling away those who were in the way, the strongest among us quickly found our way up into the train. Those who didn't or couldn't fight their way up, remained on the ground. I never heard so many curses in one place in so many languages or saw so many fists and elbows in motion. One thing was certain: in this crowd my sister and I had no chance of boarding the train by ourselves. Then suddenly an angel appeared in the form of a Russian soldier. He asked my sister what she was waiting for. She pointed to the milling crowd, and he understood her situation. He also noticed that she was with me. He took the bundles we were holding, whistled once and another soldier appeared. Each one of them picked us up by the waist and just climbed on the steps and walked up into the train without pushing and shoving. The people respected the Russian soldiers, the liberators, and made a place for them. No doubt they also envied us the privilege and honor bestowed on us by the soldiers. Then I realized our problems had just begun.

In the train, the soldiers positioned themselves right next to us, in fact a little too close to us. Instead of making us feel more secure, they alarmed us with their closeness. From our short acquaintance with Russian soldiers, we had learned that there was one thing on their mind, *dzievushkies*, girls. They were hungry for girls. Because they were our liberators, some of our girls saw fit to satisfy their needs. But my sister and I were different. We appreciated what they had done, but we weren't ready to pay their price for it. Now, unexpectedly we found ourselves in hot water. We had to scheme our way out of this situation.

Here, our knowledge of Hebrew came to our assistance. While joking with them in our broken Russian, we threw in a word or expression in Hebrew, by which we communicated between ourselves. We agreed to get off the train at the first opportunity. The soldiers of course didn't realize what we were up to. At the next stop, under the pretext of natural needs, we got off the train; first my sister, then I. We hid behind some ruins a distance from the tracks. From there we noticed the two soldiers step down and start to look for us, then the train gave a whistle, they jumped back on and away they were carried without us.

When the train was gone, my sister and I went back to the station, sat on the ground and waited, hoping for luck and another train to come.

At least this station wasn't crowded. There were only a few other people waiting. Few trains passed through the village we were in, and these were mostly freight trains carrying coal.

After a couple of hours, a freight train loaded to the brim with coal pulled into the station. I tried to figure out how we could board it. But my sister already had the solution. Before I knew it, she was sitting on top of a pile of coal. The coal was not in chunks, but like gravel. There was a ladder to climb up on, and when I reached the top of the freight car, I scampered to the top of the black pile and sat down beside my sister. We were comfortable until the train started to move. As the train moved, the pile slowly shifted. We didn't have anything to hold on to. We had to change from a sitting position to a lying one hugging the black gravely mass.

The train made few stops. I wasn't concerned with the danger we were in, of the possibility that we might slip off the pile when the train came to a sudden stop. I was too happy thinking about our destination and the possibility that we would see father soon. After riding many hours we arrived at Lodz.

Now we had to confront reality. What if father was not waiting for us? What if he had perished in the last few months before the liberation? The first thing to do was look for answers.

• • •

Lodz was a city which had vibrated with Jewish life. On Piotrokowska Street, where from Thursday afternoon till early Friday afternoon one had to struggle to get through the intersections of Polodniowa Cegelniana, the Narutowicza Streets, a constant stream of Jews had rushed to and fro. Now these streets were almost dead. I felt like a stranger in a strange city.

The first place we headed for was the *Yiddishe Gemino*. This was the center where all Jewish survivors from the concentration camps came and registered. Aside from the formal registration, all the walls in that office were covered with names scribbled in Yiddish, Polish, and Hebrew, names of searchers and those being sought, with fathers' and mothers' names. Murals with names, their birthplace and their residences, to establish positive identification.

We spent a full day there reading the walls but to no avail. None of the names were familiar to us. The next day, both of us started to approach people, asking them if they knew, had heard of, or seen father. If we saw a familiar face, we came forward, asking, "Did you see father? Don't you remember seeing father?" And if we didn't know the person, we gave descriptions and signs. But nobody remembered seeing him and nobody had heard of him. After a full week of searching and asking, we decided it was time to go to our old apartment.

With pounding hearts we drew near the intersection of Pilsudskiego and Kammienna Street. The physical appearance of the neighborhood had not changed. No destruction, no ruins. The streets, the sidewalks, the traffic, the stores, the vendors, the houses and the courtyards, were as if nothing had happened, as if there had been no war, destruction, no catastrophe. People were laughing, children were playing, carefree.

The gateway to our courtyard was wide open as it had always been at this time of day. Karol, our superintendent, was standing with his large broom in hand and talking to the superintendent of the next house, just as he had used to do.

Nothing about our courtyard had changed except that it was now devoid of children. No children played by the board-covered well. As small children we had fought for a place in order to play *stroolkies*, a game played with five little stones in which you threw one stone in the air and picked up another from the board, and so on, stone after stone, until you had all five stones in your palm. You needed two people for this game. So you had to wait till two places were available at the well, where at least two dozen children always played. Now the board was clean and shiny. No chalked names, no shouts and cries. Only silence. Deadly silence. *Where is Chanka, with whom I liked to play so much? And where is Yossie, with whom I always fought for a seat? He always claimed it had been reserved for somebody else, and that somebody else never came. But he was strong, and after losing the fight a couple of times and ending up hurt, I didn't argue with him any more.*

Standing in that courtyard I was back in my childhood, and the children and all the games of that time were so vivid and so real in my mind that I was ready to pick up the fight with Yossie and show him that he didn't have to win always. I was strong now, and could force my way into that place he held for "somebody else."

My sister nudged me out of my dream. I saw her as in a haze. She didn't look real to me. It took me some time to return to myself.

Following her gaze, I found myself looking up at our three windows. They were covered with thin pastel-color drapes. Between the drawn drapes and the windows were our beautiful pink *rolleten*, our heavy sun drapes. I remembered when our red-painted wooden floors were freshly polished, and the sun filtered through these drapes, and put a golden shine on the floor then the whole room was filled with a sunny happiness. But the most intense impression of my early childhood days was the *Erev Pesach* day, the day of the first seder night, when everything had to be changed, made new and fresh, everything had to glisten and sparkle. Even the walls had to be painted.

I saw myself lying on the white embroidered bedspread, on my mother's bed. I was enjoying *Gan-Eden*, Paradise. No one was equal to me, and no one could take me off that bed. I made myself sleep. The rule in our family was never to wake somebody from his or her sleep. I took full advantage of that rule.

Who is behind those drapes now? And who takes my place on my mother's bed? The mere thought of my mother filled me with such a longing that I felt my life begin to spin around. It was hyptnotic. I simply could not tear myself away. I was engulfed in my past. I started to tremble all over as vision after vision whirled around kaleidoscopically before my mind's eye. My father sitting at the head of the table, my mother, sitting at the other end, facing her "king." At the *seder* the husband is king, and the wife is the queen. Proud and full of pleasure, my mother checks to see if all the traditional dishes are in their right places. She notices that I put on the white collar, the new lace one that she ran out to buy me at the last minute this afternoon. I see the slight nod with her head, and I know that she is satisfied. I did not forget to put it on, although I chattered with my friend till the last minute before lighting the candles. Everything is in order. Everybody is in his holiday dress. The *kittle*, (a man's solemn white linen robe which the Jew wears to the *seder* as well as on Atonement Day), ah, what a beautiful kittel, how happy mother is that her Reuven Yosef listened to her and bought himself such a beautiful kittel.

My father, the "king," his face shining, also checks the arrangements. He is also pleased. His *Aishet Chayill* (Woman of Valor) did not forget to prepare the salt water, the hard boiled eggs, the romaine lettuce. How did she get romaine lettuce at this time of the year? But that is his Esther, as always proving the impossible can be done if one tries hard enough. And the *Ke'arah*? How beautifully she had prepared this traditional plate, with each ingredient exactly in its right place. He looks at his "queen" across the long table and his happiness is written all over his face; his pride, his tranquility are all thanks to her. In the lovely new light green satin dress she is wearing she is absolutely enchanting. Now he turns his gaze toward us. His eyes are full of approval and joy. I can feel the pleasure he derives from seeing us. Then he turns his eyes slowly and with dignity to his left and to his right, where his father and his father-in-law are seated. With his eyes he seems to say, "I've got heaven on earth; can I ask for more?" Both my grandfathers read his silent message, and with their glances show their pleasure at his gratification.

As these images wheeled before my eyes, I turned against myself, hating myself for the weakness that chose illusion to the reality I had come to find. Then, my sister pointed at our home. I saw a man standing behind the window drapes. He saw us staring at him and seemed to be angry. There was no way but to go up and explain.

"Who is there?" a hoarse voice answered my knock at the door. Neither of us answered. The man opened the door, just wide enough to look at our faces and asked: "What do you want?" I didn't look at his face, I looked behind him, and once again, painful memories rolled back to a vanished past.

The furniture and the pictures were still the same. They even were in the same places they had been before we left our house. The color of the walls was still the same. Nothing had changed; yet everything was changed. I heard the door shut with great force, and I stared at its blankness for several minutes.

Hurt and shamed, I grasped my sister's hand. With broken hearts and trembling feet, we went down the staircase.

Outside, in the courtyard Karol was sweeping the paved ground. He looked at us and crossed himself twice. "Are you alive? They said that both of you were killed. So what do you want here?" Karol said.

In the street we looked at each other. We fell into each other's embrace, and burst into tears. After a while we wiped each other's tears and started to walk. But we had no place to go to. The home of our happy childhood was gone. Our family was gone. Our past was wiped out. We walked for a while in silence. Then we turned to each other and asked:

"Where is father now?"

9. Aftermath

Is this reality or is it a mirage? Is this freedom or a concentration camp all over again? My head was spinning.

Nineteen hundred and forty-seven: at long last I was standing on friendly soil. Then why were we surrounded by a tall wire fence?

I was in Israel, but I wasn't liberated yet. The enclosure was real.

I do not know how long it took me to accept that this was not a dream, not a fantasy or fiction. I was free indeed, and this earth I was standing on was positively the land of Israel. But the country wasn't free yet, Israel was still occupied by the British.

For us, the people who came by boat from Cyprus, the British detention camp was another link in a long chain of camps. For us undergoing a three-month quarantine period, this was the last bearing of the heavy yoke of our long and dark exile. This camp had been especially erected for people like us, people who had cheated death and survived the Nazis.

It was as if the British said: "Why should we make it easy for you? We didn't ask you to survive." When they detected our refugee boat on the high seas, they surrounded it with two gigantic military ships. They escorted us to Haifa. We saw the flickering lights of Mount Carmel. They then forced us to disembark onto their ship and brought us to Cyprus. After being detained for almost a year there, they brought us here to the quarantine camp, in Atlit.

Atlit was one gigantic prison with separate quarters for men and women. Even married couples could see each other only during the day. The British did not let the people forget that they were prisoners under surveillance. The inmates counted every day that passed for each day brought them closer to freedom in the land of Israel.

I arrived in Atlit from Cyprus with a teen group of six hundred youngsters. That morning the sun had climbed high in the sky. But brighter than the sun was the joy in my heart knowing that with the end of Atlit would come the end of exile and wandering. Here I was standing on the threshhold of a new world, with new hopes for the future. I fell to the ground and kissed the earth. The white warm sand felt so sweet and soft and peaceful that I desired to take it with me and make it my own. I lost any sense of time in that marvelous moment of enchantment. But it ended when a man took me gently by the hand and brought me over to the others who were waiting for me to join them.

Through a tall wire gate we were led to a site where there were no pavements or streets. There was only hot white sand, wooden barracks, and shiny, tall wire fences. Behind those fences were people, people on whose faces one could read anxiety and sorrow.

For these people were searching for familiar faces among the new arrivals. A year and half after the war had ended, they still hoped to find their loved ones. Their expectation intensified with each disappointment. Here and there one could see eyes filled with tears. All of the people were standing on their toes, their outstretched necks turning to and fro, studying and seeking recognition in every new face. Every once in a while one of them would jump up in anticipation and call out a name. But as soon as he uttered the name he would take on a look of disappointment when the person he had called to came to the fence. The commotion and tumult were beyond description.

In the midst of the appealing calls, encouraging shouts, and bewildered responses, my heart leaped into my throat. *Oh G-d! Make this be true! Make it real! Do not dash my dream! Not this one!*

We were looking into each other's eyes. We opened our mouths to call out to each other, but no sounds came out. Words had disappeared into some unknown dimension. We communicated in a sudden burst of tears. Our hearts were full and our eyes overfull. Nothing could stop our tears. We could not control ourselves. We tried to kiss through the wire fence. It was awkward, but even so I didn't mind. I knew it was she. I saw that she was alive, *Doda* Bluma, my dearest aunt.

We wanted to embrace, but the tall wire fence was in our way. Our tears spoke more clearly than any language. Next to my aunt stood a tall, handsome man. He made me uncomfortable. I thought him tactless. He intruded on our privacy. He just stood there and examined me with his beautiful large brown eyes, which made me feel embarrassed. Then without interrupting his study of me, he handed me a handkerchief. My aunt introduced him as her husband. Now I looked at him searchingly. This was not the uncle I knew. Then I remembered that my uncle had died in the ghetto. Oh! So this must be my aunt's second husband.

Not only was my new uncle tall and handsome, he was also a most gentle man. He soon won my confidence. The tender smile never left his lips and his eyes had a kind of amiable, soft expression which invited trust. He left us alone for a couple of minutes and came back after receiving permission from the guard to take me inside the fence. I followed my aunt and uncle to a wooden hut, where about fity women lived together; each of them had a bed, a night table, and a doorless linen closet.

Immediately my aunt started to barrage me with questions. Had I heard anything of my father? When did I see him last? Did I know if he left Auschwitz? Did I know where he was sent after Auschwitz? I did not blame her for wanting to know. But I couldn't provide her with satisfying answers; I had to leave most of her questions unanswered. Both of us knew that if my father was alive we would have heard from him. Now all hope for her brother was lost. She left the hut.

When my new uncle and I were left alone, he drew out a picture from her linen closet and said in a trembling voice: "Anna! Please, have pity and hide this picture so that she will never see it again." I looked at it and recognized my two little cousins: Alusia, five years old, and Ryvcia, three years old. While I looked at these little children in the photograph, my uncle told me that my aunt had obtained the picture from London. The first time she saw it she went into shock; she had had to be hospitalized and put under sedation for a few days. Now, whenever she looked at them she became faint. I felt her pain and I sensed his dilemma. I put the white envelope containing the picture in the pocket of my dress.

When my aunt returned she seemed more relaxed. She told me how she and my uncle had met in Italy after the war ended. Then she started to talk about herself. She walked over to the linen closet and started to look for something. Disappointed, she said: "I have something to show you, but where is it? I must have misplaced it. Some other time perhaps." I showed no reaction; however, the issue wasn't closed. She became emotional and restless. She sat down near me, took my hand into her palm, and started to play with my fingers, without looking at them or at me. She became lost in her thoughts. We sat thus for about ten minutes when I noticed tears running down her cheeks. Then in a trembling, almost convulsive voice, she said to herself: "Do you know, Anna, that here right next to you sits a murderer, a mother, a murderer of her own two little babies!" I wanted to say something but she didn't let me interrupt. "Do not contradict me please! I know it and nobody will convince me otherwise until I die." She then turned her back to me, and staring into the distance became lost in her thoughts again.

In 1942 a wild epidemic of dysentery had engulfed the whole Lodz ghetto. Every second house was quarantined. My aunt's two children caught the disease. Being afraid to send them to a hospital because of the constant deportations, my aunt kept them at home and tried to minister to them herself. She had been reluctant to call in a doctor, for he would have put them immediately in the hospital. But when the children became dehydrated and she saw that they would die, she had no choice but to seek professional help. So the children were put in one of the nearest hospitals. The following morning our ghetto was shocked with the greatest tragedy imaginable: all the hospitals were emptied of their patients, including the children from the pediatric wards. Among them were Alusia and Ryvcia.

When the ghetto woke to that catastrophe, the despair of the people was overwhelming. Mothers ran after trucks, seeking their children. They wept and tore their hair. Many jumped on the trucks with the hope that they might find them there or wherever they were being taken to.

Doda Bluma ran after each truck she saw, hoping that she would recognize her children among those passing. Then at an intersection a truck full of children sped by. She did not see them but she recognized the desperate weak voices: "*Mamusiu! Ratuj nas! Ratuj! Ratuj! Ratuj nas!*" (Mommy, save us! Save us! Save us!) She saw their small outstretched hands. She ran after the truck. Suddenly a sondercommando threw her to the cobblestone pavement and she lost consciousness.

My aunt lost both of her children to the flames, smoke and ashes of German death factories. She, however, survived to see the end of the Holocaust. Until the day she died, she felt guilty for not being strong or fast enough to snatch her children from the moving truck. She accused herself of being a "murderer of her own children" because she had allowed the children to be put in the hospital. She never forgave herself for not following her children to the crematorium.

I do not know how she handled the loss of the picture. She never mentioned the subject to me. However, afterwards, whenever she came to my house she always seemed to find an excuse to rearrange my furniture. My apartment was on the ground floor, with windows facing a garden. Once, when I was tending some bushes in the garden I glanced through the window and noticed my aunt slowly going through my closet, carefully shaking out my linens piece by piece. I stood up and watched her open all my drawers. She opened every envelope she found and unfolded every piece of paper. I started to cry. I knew that she was looking for the image of her two lost children.

• • •

Now free, free of the Nazis, I became enslaved to memories which evoked a thousand questions. I became obsessed in my search for answers. Where and how did my father die? Was he beaten or gassed to death? Was he burned alive? Why did I survive, while my brother and mother and father perished? Was I better than they were? Was I more pious than they? No! Then, why, why, why? It is said that time is the best healer. It is forty years now since our tragedy began, yet my wounds have not healed.

How to adjust to life became another problem. My desire to go on living left me when I realized that my father would never return. The difficulty then of beginning a new life was made harder by the irreconcilable gap I found between the survivors and those who had not been singed by the Nazi flames. They could not relate to our feelings and seemed not to hear what we had to say. When we tried to enter life in a normal fashion, not a life limited to survivors only, we had to resort to silence. We did not talk of our past.

Yet we were asked painful questions. What could one answer when he or she was asked, "Why didn't you escape?" "Why didn't you fight like those in the Warsaw ghetto?" Or worse yet: "How come you survived and not your mother, or brother, or father?" I became speechless when I heard such questions. I wasn't prepared for such lack of understanding and such ignorance on the part of those who had not suffered. I tried to explain, as best as I could, what had happened in those days. But my stories of what I went through sounded incredible to my listeners; they simply could not believe them. They thought that I was inventing. They could not believe that people were burned alive, were gassed, were buried in ditches, still breathing, after being shot and wounded. How could one explain to those who were not there that some fathers ate up their infants' portions of bread, assuring the babies' deaths, while others gave away their last crusts to their children, condemning themselves to death in a very short span of time.

"Why didn't you escape?" A reasonable question. But escape to where? Who would take you in? Who wanted to help? Certainly not the majority of gentiles, who were in a position to help. They were threatened with loss of their own lives if they hid a Jew; on the other hand they were rewarded if they disclosed the hideout of a Jew. What often happened was that the gentiles took all the possessions of the Jews, on the promise that they would hide them or their children, but they did not keep their promises and gave both parents and children over to the Gestapo.

It was too much for the Holocaust victim to explain, to try to make people understand and believe. Hurt to the core of one's being, one withdrew from that subject, from telling people in America what had happened in Europe. One left it to history to explain and give answers.

Still the questons continued. "Why didn't you revolt?" People did not try to understand that when we faced the machine guns our heroism was muted. Weren't there millions of heroic defenders of Stalingrad and Moscow, not Jews, who died and were shot in the camps without trying to revolt? Now, to sit and to judge the victims in retrospect was more than the survivor could take. It is a great wonder that every survivor did not become bitter at the whole world.

"How did you survive, and not the others?" The question implied one had survived at somebodyelse's expense. Was it possible to convince people that those who survived had had no hand in their own survival? They were not smarter than others, they were not more ingenious, more gifted, or more skillful than the others. They survived by sheer chance, by miracles not because they were heroes or heroines. Heroes were killed on the spot. If spitting in an SS man's face was a heroic act, then those who acted so heroically left it to others to tell their stories. They themselves did not survive.

Just as the blunting of emotions was a necessary psychological protection which enabled the survivor of the concentration camps to go on living, so, too, repressing the memory of the past was necessary for the survivor to rebuild his or her life anew, in a normal society and in normal conditions. However, no matter how much the memory of that hellish existence was repressed, it could not be entirely buried. Certain wounds never healed.

There are many well-meaning people who would like to know, would like to understand, how I felt when I was deprived of everything they would consider normal. They try to imagine, vicariously, how we survived in the hell of ghettos and concentration camps, and to do so they ask questions. They don't know that their questions throw me back to an era which I have pushed away into the farthest corner of my mind.

So it happened with Isaac Rosen. It was an innocent discussion—at least on his part. He was trying to justify the Israeli government accepting money from Germany as part restitution for the wrong done to the Jews in World War II. His argument was that the Israeli government needed the money to restore her economy. "The money will make Israel prosper," he said.

But I could not agree with him. "If Israel accepts the money, the Germans will have their consciences eased. The Germans will have acquitted for themselves, their children, and future generations. How can blood be repaid with money?" I asked him. "The most prosperous economy cannot restore the spilled blood of innocent people who were silenced in the prime of life. It is their honor we should concern ourselves with. They left a legacy and we must not betray them. Taking money from the Germans would be to betray them, the *Keddoshim*; accepting money for their blood will make a mockery of their innocent deaths."

Isaac Rosen was too stubborn and my arguments did not convince him—he considered himself to be an expert on the subject. He smiled a winner's smile, but I was burning inside. I left his house and went home. I went about my everyday business and chores, but the self-assured voice of Isaac followed me everywhere I went. Day and night I heard it. It gave me no peace. It raised so many questions and opened so many wounds.

One evening, after we had just finished supper, my older son Yossi went to the counter in the kitchen, picked up a little white pot, and started to eat out of it. (It contained some rice and beef stew, a dish for him just in case he got hungry.) When I saw him standing with the small pot close to his mouth and eating out of it, I let out a scream: "What are you doing? What are you doing?" I yelled, and then I started to cry. I cried and cried and cried and he didn't know why. Nobody saw what I saw in that little white pot. The madness of Auschwitz rose before me again in all its dehumanizing brutality, and the calendar turned back a full twenty-five years.

I was in block thirty-one. We were being punished. For three days we couldn't leave the block; we were given nothing to eat those three days. I was lying on the *pritch* with four other girls. The *pritches* were so low that I, though only five feet tall, couldn't sit up straight. All of us were sitting with our heads bent. After the third day we were given soup to eat. The soup for us five girls was brought to us in one big white pot. A fifteen-quart pot! I was handed this pot, for I was sitting nearest to the aisle. I looked into the pot and saw that five portions hardly covered its bottom. I was holding a lifesaving treasure and I didn't know what to do with it. There was no spoon. So I lifted the pot up high with the intention of spilling some of the soup in my mouth. But no sooner had I done so when one of the other girls grabbed the pot from my hands.

She also tried to eat but was equally unsuccessful. She threw herself on her back, lifted the pot with both her hands, and let the soup flow into her mouth. At that moment the three other girls threw themselves on the pot, too. They started to devour the soup with their hands. As I watched them eat, my stomach turned. They looked like a pack of hungry dogs fighting over a bone someone had thrown them. I started to cry, more from shame than hunger. Only then did the other girls remember me. They looked in the pot. There was still some soup left. As one, all of them let go of the pot and handed it to me. But no matter how hard I tried, I could not bring myself to put my hand inside it and take out the watery soup. I felt that if I started eating with my hands, I would choke.

The girls were good girls and tried to help. They made me cup my palms, and then slowly turned the pot to let the remaining soup flow into them. I started to sip from my cupped palms. While I was doing that one of the girls held her palm underneath mine to catch the spilled drops, while another girl licked drops from her dirty blanket. I did not know if even one of those girls survived the war. I just knew that this scene, like many others, remained engraved in my mind forever.

After this scene of shame and debasement came back to me in my own beautiful home twenty-five years later, it took me more than a week of sleepless nights to bring myself to resume my normal life.

Can people who did not go through the Holocaust understand what goes on in our minds? Even when we laugh and try to be jolly? Can they understand our inner conflicts, feel what we struggle with in the darkness of the night when we try to bring back memories, or struggle to forget them? Whenever I think back to the horrible days of the Nazi era, I try, often quite instinctively, to analyze the behavior of other people as well as my own. This is not to sit in judgement of acts committed or refrained from. It is also not an act of curiosity. It is, rather, trying to understand the actions in retrospect. With regard to myself in particular, it seems that if I can find the right justification for a deed, I may achieve some relief from my self-condemnation. This feeling was present in me when I first met with Bluma after a separation of twenty-five years.

We were reminiscing. She spoke of the long nights we used to work in the resort. She recalled Ludka, how delicate and slow were her movements while eating, in contrast to the gulping that we used to do. Bluma told me how desperately she tried to imitate Ludka, but always without success. Bluma had been so hungry. I explained to her that Ludka was never as hungry as we were because she had *protekcja*, (pull) in the ghetto. She also had a mother who ran the house. Once, when I passed her apartment, I looked into the window. I saw the table set, just as before the war. I saw wine on the table, even an apple, yes, a real apple! It was standing there in a real fruit dish. Who could imagine an apple in the ghetto or a bottle of wine? For Ludka there was no hunger, I told Bluma. Ludka, after wine and apples, could slowly eat her soup. When I thought of Ludka now, I wondered that she could eat our soup at all. She could afford to be delicate in her manners. But for Bluma these facts didn't justify her own conduct. "We were like animals," she said. "And that is exactly what Hitler wanted to make of us," I answered.

After a while I got the feeling that she had tried very hard to repress the thought of her own behavior in the ghetto. She also tried to justify it, explaining that she was still a child, that she didn't know how to act properly in relation to the other members of her family, and therefore that she often acted childishly and thoughtlessly. When I asked her if she was speaking in regard to my father, she completely denied it. She said that she was talking in general terms. To me it looked as though she was trying to evade the issue.

The issue of hunger and the handling of it opens a deep wound in me, especially when I think of those many years I used to blame Bluma for letting me be led into heartbreaking confrontations with father. The issue was the suspicion of injustice provoked by "lust" in touching a crumb of bread that did not belong to him, or taking a grain of sugar that did not belong to him. All these "transgressions" burn like fire now. No one who did not live through the experience can really understand it. Oh, she wasn't the only one who made "signs" in her portion of the sugar, or measured her portion of bread with a string to see if someone had touched it, or painted a line on the tiny jar of oil to make sure that no tongue had touched it. The most terrible thing was that one felt so degraded doing such things; yet one could not help oneself. One was as if under a spell, fully realizing that these acts expressed a loss of human dignity. The shame and disgrace one felt while the mental struggle was going on was agonizing torture; yet the pangs of hunger overpowered everything. One acted according to one's instinct and a blind desire to live.

And now, after over forty years, I dare to think that maybe now I can analyze that period when days turned into nights and my soul was torn apart and my sleep was filled with nightmares.

When I first unburdened my troubles to my aunt, I thought that my nightmares would subside. They did in fact do so, but they kept on returning. Now, as a mature person, I comprehend why I still feel remorse, although more than forty years have gone by, for I cannot correct the wrong I did to my father because my father never returned.

I always thought and hoped that if I could talk them out with my sister I would be relieved of my guilt feelings. But I became aware that, consciously or unconsciously, my sister tried to avoid the subject. She supressed the issue. Once, when she was talking about my father, I cautiously asked if she had some guilt feelings or remorse about him. She answered, "No," and that was that. I, for my part, cannot understand how she could have dismissed such an important matter. Had she forgotten that she had urged me to have an open confrontation with father? Was she wrong or was she right? Was father right or was he wrong? I could not answer.

It is well known by now that Hitler was obsessed with the question of the Jews. He not only set the pattern of how they were to die, but also the pattern of how they were to live before they died. And just as he designed his tortures for the body, he designed tortures for the soul. In creating inhuman living conditions, he forced the lowest character traits to emerge from the sufferer and killed the essence of humanity in him. One of the most fundamental wrongs the unbearable circumstances did was to set sister against sister, brother against brother, child against father, and even child against mother. The cause was the torturous hunger the victims wrestled with in the ghetto and in the concentration camps. I cannot liberate myself from my conscience, from accusing myself that I wronged my own father.

I cannot say in all honesty that by criticizing my sister I alleviated my problem in the least. Had I been right in blaming her all these years, or was it that both of us were victims, the tools of the Nazi policy? The thing that happened to me, happened in almost the same fashion to my best friend Judith.

We grew up together, matured together, and suffered the same fate together during the war years. Because of circumstances, when we could not live together, we lived close to each other. When both of us got married, we still remained the best of friends. Each of us created her own kingdom in her private life.

I knew that Judith was suffering as all of us survivors suffered. I also knew that it was comforting to unload the weight on one's heart to someone who understood. But she had a different philosophy. Her burden was for herself alone and not for others.

Time did not stand still. One generation was born, another generation died. One year followed the other, and in time young girls turned into grandmothers. But Judith did not change, or so it seemed. She had the same smile, the same readiness to help, the same willingness to sacrifice for others, the same soft shoulder to lean on no matter who needed it, until she lost her husband.

Judith and I had a world in common but not a common philosophy. I never liked to keep anger inside of me. Before my anger had a chance to cool I had to express it. If I found I was wrong, then I apologized. Judith, however, was different. She was always under control. I envied this trait in her. I looked at her as a tower of strength. Therefore I was taken aback when one evening she declared that she had a need to talk to me, that she wanted to confide something that weighed heavily on her.

That evening another Judith revealed herself to me.

"We were walking on the crackling snow," she said. "The first rays of the spring sun were out, and it looked as if the snow would melt that day. I felt an emptiness mixed with hope for another spring, and maybe another summer. But what would this spring or summer bring with it? Changes? Would our freedom come with the new seasons?

"In my deepest consciousness, I did not believe that freedom would ever come; however, I felt strongly that I would survive. Who gave me that feeling of assurance? My father. I felt that as long as my sister and I had my father's presence, we would survive. He was our protector and our spiritual strength. He was the authority in the house, but at the same time he was interested in the smallest detail of our lives. When we needed his understanding, he gave it. Therefore, when my sister suggested keeping our rations separate I was startled.

"As long as my mother and brother lived, we never kept our rations separate. Mother used to cut one slice of bread for each of us—the first slice she gave to my father, the next slice to my brother, the next to me and the next to my sister. She divided the bread equally for everyone; then she gave to my father more from her portion, saying she did not need that much food. If he did not accept the additional bread, she would not eat at all. She knew my father needed more food, for he was a big man, and she did not want to deprive us of what little was apportioned to us. We needed the bread, too. But she thought she could do with less, and she couldn't stand to see my father suffer hunger.

"My mother died of malnutrition. My brother succumbed to typhoid fever at the height of the epidemic that swept the ghetto in 1942.

"My sister and I worked in the Straw Resort. We braided straw to make straw shoes for German soldiers. Every second week we had night shifts. That day we were walking on the crackling snow because we had an hour and a half before our shift started. My sister had suggested the walk. Had I known what this walk would bring I would have refused to go.

"We were talking about different things when my sister stopped and said she wanted to talk about food. What about food? What was there to talk about, I wondered. 'There is no other way to get food except the way we receive rations now,' I said.

" 'I do not mean that,' my sister said. 'I mean the way we distribute it among us.' I guessed what she meant, but I did not answer and she went on. 'I feel that we should divide the rations separately, the way everybody does.' 'What about father?' I asked. 'The same share should go to father as goes to us. We are getting so little that it is not right to have less than we are entitled to.'

"I did not like the idea, but I should not have been shocked to hear what my sister was saying. During the past few months she had made remarks about the unequal division of food among us, but she had not spoken as plainly as she did now.

"'What do you want me to do? Father needs more food than we do.' I said. But she did not agree with me. She stated her arguments, which were valid, why we should divide the rations when we got them. When I got my share of bread in the morning, about four or six ounces, I ate it up all at once because I was so hungry. From the morning till night and even during the night I thought of nothing else but my hunger. My father, too, did likewise, but my sister had the will power to keep from eating her slice all at once. She was able to divide her bread into portions! She would eat a piece in the morning, then a piece in the afternoon, and in the evening she still had half of her slice for supper. By then, my father and I were ravenous. The sight of her bread, and the sense of not being able to have it, drove me crazy. And I am sure that my father felt the same way.

"My sister was a good-hearted girl; she could not stand to see us suffer. So she either divided her supper portion into three—sharing with us what she had saved so that none of us was starving before going to bed—or she allowed us to take a paper-thin slice of bread from her next day's portion. This went on every single day, and almsot every day she shared with us.

"But in all honesty, my sister's sharing did not help us much. And in whatever way we acted, we wronged her. She was the one who suffered: we took her last crumb of bread and hated ourselves for doing it. I could not look at my own face in the mirror or into my own heart.

"It often happened that we did not have bread for four or five days at a stretch. I did not know where she hid it, but before going to bed she somehow came up with a bit of bread, nevertheless. I can still see her outstretched hand, with a tiny piece of bread in it. Oh, how I wished I could knock this morsel from her palm. But I could not. Despite my abhorring it, I could not bring myself to do that. The morsel was too precious. It would have been insane to waste it. Can you understand this dilemma, this struggle of a hunger-torn soul?

"My sister was an angel. I knew it then, and I know it now. However, in those hellish days, when she spoke to me about the idea of dividing the bread from the beginning, she showed me a mirror into which I should have looked long before. I had conveniently taken advantage of her goodness, of her charitable heart. Now, I had no argument with which to dispute her request. I was confused, ashamed and angry at myself. I did not know how to respond. She argued her position, point after point, and I listened and felt guilty.

"My guilt feelings were beyond measure. I let myself be persuaded by her. I think that this was the only time she ever persuaded me in a really important matter. I wish I had realized then how important it was. If I had, I would not have spent the rest of my life hating myself for listening to her.

"On that walk with my little sister, I agreed to talk to father about the matter. As we came into the room—our home in the ghetto consisted of one small room—father was sitting and reading. He looked up and asked us if we had had a nice walk. I said yes, and started to tell him about my sister's idea without saying it was hers. After two sentences, I realized the mistake I had made. Father just looked at me. I can still see that look on my father's face as he said: '... dividing the bread... my little girl gives both of us the last morsel from her mouth.'

"Father just gazed at me and his eyes grew larger and larger and filled with tears. The tears rolled one by one, down his cheeks. I wanted to take my words back, but they had been spoken, and they would resound in my head till the end of my life.

"I felt then as I know now that there was no repentance for my sin of hurting my dear father. I fell on his chest. I asked for forgiveness. He cried, he placed both his hands over my head. Then with his right hand he lifted my face. He kissed my forehead, pressing me against his breast as he continued weeping, and he rocked me back and forth. I burst into a loud wail; he too was wailing. Then he gently pushed me a little away from him, dried my tears and said, 'Stop! It is enough.'

"He called my sister, embraced and kissed her and ordered her to stop crying also. It was only then that I realized that she too was sobbing. Then he sat down, took us both on his lap—as he used to do when we were little kids—and said in his strict voice, 'From now on, we will divide our rations.'

"Both my sister and I opened our mouths simultaneously. 'No! No protesting,' he said. 'The war will be over soon. We will have enough bread. We will even have butter! We will have enough to eat, but till then, till then, we need patience, patience my children.'

"We tried to protest again, but to no avail. Father did not give in. From then on, we apportioned our bread and whatever else we received for rations as he had said.

"I now have enough bread and butter and enough of everything else. I am also a mother and know that father forgave me. But I have never been able to forgive myself for the words I uttered so foolishly. I never forgave and I will never forget it. My father never came back and my words still haunt my memory. I can still hear them as I spoke them in the darkness of that night."

Like Judith, I have tried to suppress certain memories so as to be able to go on living a normal life. However, from time to time, the hell of my past has violently leaped to life again, as happened one time in a classroom.

A teacher at Talmudic University was interpreting the enslavement of the Jews in Egypt, as follows: "The Jews in Egypt were enslaved not only physically and spiritually, but their ability to think and make judgements was also destroyed." Since I see almost everything from the perspective of the Holocaust, I responded: "Just like the Jews in Europe. Hitler took away our freedom, physically and spiritually. However, he could not destroy our power to think and . . ." Before I had a chance to finish, the teacher picked up my statement and twisted it to conform to his own line of thought: "Yes you are right. The European Jews lost their ability to think and to evaluate. When they saw the Holocaust coming upon them, they did not stop to analyze why such a great misfortune befell them. They did not comprehend and did not see that this happened to them because they were sinners. The European Jews were steeped in sin, and the Holocaust was a punishment for their sins." No arrow cut sharper, and no fire burned hotter than his statement did. For a moment I lost my voice.

I wanted to answer but I was speechless. His words had cut my throat like a knife. But I couldn't let him get away with his explanation, and at last I said: "Were the European Jews more sinful than the American Jews? Were the European *Zaddikim* and our pious Rabbis sinful? And the million children, for whose sin were they punished?" His answer was short and sharp: "The European Jews had the ability to do better. They had models. America is a young country. They don't have the models the European Jews had."

After class I went to his office. "Granted," I said, "that you have a direct line to our Lord and you know that our *Zaddikim* were sinners, can you please tell me why my brother died while I survived? He was a young and pious boy, he did not want to defile himself with *treif*, he did not want to eat the horse meat which could have saved his life. He who studied Torah all his young life died, while I, who ate treif, survived? Was I better than he was? Was he the sinner and I the righteous?'' I walked out without waiting for his answer. I felt that I was losing control over my senses.

Sleepless nights and restless days followed this experience. I functioned normally, yet I felt caged. And one long night full of tossings and turnings I realized that a large part of my torment was the product of memories locked in me. That night I decided that the only way to resolve my problem was to commit my memories to writing, to break my silence.

This sudden realization triggered some dormant mechanism inside me. I suddenly felt an urge to scream, to tell my truth. How we, the Jews of Europe, lived before the catastrophe, and how we died in the Nazi hell. All those who were there know that it is impossible with words to express the extent of our tragedy—the greatest in Jewish history—for it is beyond human possibility to do so. When we talk about the Holocaust, the words we use do not convey the reality of it, the meaning of it. The word "hunger" had a different meaning for us in the ghetto and in the concentration camp than it has for one who was never there. And so is it with many other words we use. Therefore the story of the Holocaust can never be told in its totality, for what happened is indescribable. It is beyond human imagination. Nevertheless, I would try to tell some small part of it, one family's experience in the ghetto; and I owed it to the dead to inform the living so they would not be so quick to judge those who are no longer here to defend themselves. It is my obligation to open up their ears and minds. There is a time to be silent, and there is a time to let one's voice be heard.

Bibliography

Berkovits, Eliezer, *Faith After the Holocaust*. New York: Ktav, 1973.
Berkovits, Eliezer, *With God In Hell*. New York: Sanhedrin Press, 1979.
Borowski, Tadeusz, *This Way for the Gas, Ladies and Gentlemen*. New York: Penguin Books, 1976. Translated by Barbara Veder.
Bryks, Rachmiel, *Der Keizer in Ghetto (The King in the Ghetto)*. New York: Cyko Farlag, 1961.
Dabrowska, Danita and Dobroszycki, Lucjan, *Kronika Getta Lodzkiego (The Chronicle of the Lodz Ghetto)*. Poland: Wydawnictwo Lodzkie, 1965.
Delbo, Charlotte, *None of Us Will Return*. Boston: Beacon Press, 1968. Translated by John Githens.
Des-Pres. *The Survivor*. New York: Gulf & Western, 1977.
Frank, Anne. *The Diary of a Young Girl*. New York: 1967.
Frankl, Victor E. *Man's Search for Meaning*. New York: 1959.
Friedman, Philip. *this Was Oswiencim (Auschwitz)*. London: The United Jewish Relief Appeal, 1946.
Granatstein, Yechiel. *Fremde Welder—Eigene Erd (Foreign Forests—Own Earth)*. Tel-Aviv, Israel: Peretz Publishing, 1979.
Granatstein, Yechiel. *Hashemesh Beanan (The Sun in the Cloud)*. Jerusalem: Mosad Harav Kook, 1975.
Katznelson, Yitzhak. *Vittal Diary*. London: Ghetto Fighter's House, 1960.
Klugman, Alexander. *Ghetto Lodz*. Tel-Aviv, Israel: S. Kibel, 1964.
Kowalski, Isaac. *A Secret Press in Nazi Europe*. New York: Shengold Publishers, 1969.
Langer, Lawrence L. *Versions of Survival*. New York: State University, 1982.
Poznanski, Jakub. *Pamientnik Z Getta Lodzkiego (A Diary From the Lodz Ghetto)*. Lodz: Wydawnictwo Lodzkie, 1961.
Prager, Moshe. *Aille Shelo Nechneu (Those Who Never Yielded)*. Bne-Brak, Israel, 1961.
Prager, Moshe. *Sparks of Glory*. New York: Shengold Publishers, 1974.

Ringlebaum, Emanuel. *Notes From the Warsaw Ghetto*. New York: Shocken, 1974.

Shabbetai, K. *As Sheep to the Slaughter?* New York: Marstin Press, 1963.

Tabaksblat, Israel. *Churban Lodz (The Destruction of Lodz)*. Buenos Aires, Argentina: Union Central Israelita Polaca, 1946.

Trunk, Isaiah. *Judenrat (Jewish Councils)*. New York: Stein & Day, 1979.

Wiesel, Elie. *The Gates of the Forest*. New York: Holt, Rinehart & Winston, 1964.

Weismandel, Michoel Dov. *Min Hameitzar (From the Depths of Distress)*. Jerusalem: Hotzaat Nei Hamechaber, 1960.

Yassny, Wolf A. *The Extermination of the Lodz Jewry*. Tel-Aviv, Israel: Irgun HaLodzaim in Israel, 1950.

Zelver-Urbach, Sarah. *Lu Yehee Boker (Would It Were Morning)*. Tel-Aviv, Israel: Moreshet, 1981.

Zelver-Urbach, Sarah. *Mee Bead Lechalon Baitee (Looking Through My Window)*. Jerusalem: Yad VaShem, 1964.

Zyskind, Sarah. *Stolen Years*. Minneapolis: Lerner Pub., 1981.